Complete with
LAYOUTS FOR PLAYING

Compiled by
ALPHONSE MOYSE, Jr.

THE UNITED STATES PLAYING CARD COMPANY
At Cincinnati, Ohio, U.S.A.

*Canadian Distributors*
INTERNATIONAL PLAYING CARD COMPANY, Limited
Windsor, Ontario

# TABLE OF CONTENTS






Racine, Wisconsin Printed in U.S.A.

CONTENTS—(Continued)



# TECHNICAL TERMS

**Pack** The total number of cards used. All solitaire games use one or more standard packs of 52 cards, without jokers. When two or more packs are used, they are shuffled together.

Rank of cards in each suit, except in a few specified cases, is from low to high: A, 2, 3, 4, 5, 6, 7, 8, 9, 10, J, Q, K. In games where cards are valued numerically, they run from one to 13, ace being one, jack 11, queen 12, king 13.

In some games, ranking is circular, ace following king. This is always true if foundation cards other than aces and kings are used. The rank of foundations usually marks the end of the sequence in tableau building. For example, if 5's are foundation cards and downward building is permitted on the tableau, a 6 can be built on a 7 but not a 5 on a 6, because 5's must be played up to the foundation row.

**Layout**—The total number of cards dealt to start the game. The layout can be comprised of the following parts: foundations, tableau, stock, and reserve—although few games use all four. In this book, foundations are usually discussed separately from the rest of the layout to simplify instructions for play.

**Foundations**—Certain cards that must be segregated at some stage and built up with available cards. In any game using foundations, the objective is to build every foundation to the specified limit in order to win the game.

**Tableau**—Broadly, the rest of the layout other than foundations. Specifically, the part of the tableau on which building is permitted, auxiliary to foundation building. Tableau cards may be arranged so that faces can be seen.

**Stock**—A pile of cards dealt in the layout, which must be kept squared up so that only one at a time can be identified.

**Reserve**—A group of cards in the layout, spread like a tableau, available for foundation building but never built upon.

**Hand**—Cards remaining after the layout has been dealt. The hand must be kept face down until the cards are made available according to the rules of the various games.

**Wastepile**—A pile of cards face up, on which are placed cards from the hand not immediately available for play on the layout.

**Discard**—Cards permanently removed from play in any game.

**Deal**—The placing of cards in position for the layout. Also, the turning up of cards from the hand to make them available. In dealing the layout, place all cards face up, unless otherwise instructed.

**Redeal**—Formation and deal of a new hand. Number of redeals excludes the first layout. "Redeal twice" means run through the hand twice after the original layout. In redealing, unless otherwise instructed, pick up the wastepile and turn it over to form a new hand.

**Building**—The placing of one card upon another according to rules of the game. The rules are stated in the following terms:

**Build up:** in upward sequence of rank. (See **Pack.**)

**Build down:** in downward sequence of rank.

**Build in color:** red on red, black on black, regardless of suit.

**Build in alternate colors:** red on black, black on red, regardless of suit.

**Build in suit:** in sequence of same suit, as clubs.

**Available Card**—A card which may be lifted and moved. When rules state that the top or bottom card of a pile, column, or other group of cards is available, it should be understood that card thereby uncovered is also available.

**Row**—A horizontal line of cards parallel to the edge of the table.

**Column**—A vertical line of cards extending away from the player.

# ONE-PACK SOLITAIRES

## SIMPLE ADDITION

Grouped under this name are several solitaires of elementary character, alike in object and procedure.

**Play**—Deal a tableau as directed below. Remove cards from tableau in groups and discard. The groups must be specified face cards, or cards that make a specified total. Aces count one, and where they have any numerical value the jacks count 11, queens 12, kings 13. Fill spaces in tableau by cards from the hand. The game is won if entire pack is discarded or dealt into the tableau.

**Thirteens**—The tableau is ten cards in two rows of five. Discard kings singly and all other cards in pairs totaling thirteen.

**Elevens**—The tableau is nine cards in three rows of three. Discard jacks, queens, kings in trios of one of each rank, regardless of suits. Discard all other cards in pairs totaling eleven.

**Tens**—The tableau is thirteen cards in any convenient array. Discard 10's, jacks, queens, kings in quartets of one suit. Discard all other cards in pairs totaling ten.

**Fifteens**—The tableau is sixteen cards in four rows of four. Discard 10's, jacks, queens, kings in quartets of four of one suit. Discard all other cards in groups of any number of cards totaling fifteen.

## BLOCK SOLITAIRE

Some elementary solitaires of the Simple Addition type are played in a slightly different way.

**Play**—Deal a tableau as directed below. Continue dealing cards to cover tableau cards that total as specified. The game is won if entire pack is dealt upon tableau piles.

**Elevens**—The tableau is twelve cards in three rows of four. If face cards appear in the layout, remove and place at bottom of the pack. Fill the spaces, and continue removing face cards until all twelve cards of the layout are of lower rank than jacks.

If no face cards have been removed from the original layout, place the first face card turned up in later dealing on the bottom of the pack. (Without a face card at the bottom, the game cannot be won.)

The tableau being correct, continue dealing on it to cover cards in pairs that total eleven. When a face card is dealt, it blocks further play on that tableau pile.

**Tens**—The tableau is nine cards in three rows of three. Continue dealing to cover jacks, queens, and kings in pairs, regardless of suits, and all other cards in pairs that total ten. When a 10 is dealt, it blocks further play on that tableau pile.

# BARONESS

### (Thirteens)

Simple Addition with a difference in the manner of play.

Deal a row of five cards. Discard any kings or pairs that total thirteen. Deal five more cards on the first five, or in the spaces left by their removal. Discard as before. Continue until complete pack is dealt by rows of five, with two cards at the end which may be spread separately from the piles and are both available. Each new row of five buries the cards below in the piles until they are released by play of top cards. The game is won if the entire pack is discarded.

# FOURTEEN PUZZLE

### (Take Fourteen)

This version of Simple Addition is radically different from other members of the family. It allows fair scope for skill and does not so frequently present an unbreakable block.

Deal the pack into twelve piles face up. Put the four extra cards on the first four piles. Since all piles may and should be examined, they should be spread downward in overlapping formation.

Top cards of all piles are available. Remove available cards in pairs totaling fourteen. The game is won if all the cards can be so paired and removed.

**Helpful Hints**—If two cards totaling fourteen lie in any one pile, it is clear that the upper card must be removed with one of the three other complementary cards. Be sure to reserve one of them for this purpose. Where several piles contain such fourteens, plan how all can be resolved before making any play.

Note bottom cards of piles and lower cards generally. Where complementary cards lie at bottoms of different piles, both can be dismissed from calculation. But where the complements of a bottom card are high in other piles, it may be essential to get to this bottom card quickly in order to avoid a block.

# PYRAMID

The most popular member of the Simple Addition family. Although it rarely comes out, Pyramid is widely played and is the subject of elaborate record-keeping on the part of some devoted followers.

*Layout for Pyramid*

**Layout**—Deal twenty-eight cards in the form of a pyramid. (See diagram.) This is composed of successive rows of one to seven cards. Each card is overlapped by two cards of the row below.

A card in the pyramid is available if not covered by any other. At the outset, the seven cards of the bottom row are available. The play of two adjacent cards releases one card in the sixth row, and so on.

**Play**—From available cards, remove and discard all kings singly, and all other cards in pairs that total thirteen. (In the diagram, the following may be removed: ♦K; ♦6 and ♥7; ♠A and ♠Q; ♥8 and ♥5; ♠K; ♦9 and ♠4.

Turn up cards from the hand singly, placing unplayable cards face up on a single wastepile. The top card of this pile and the card in hand are available. Note that a card turned up from the hand may be matched with a card on the wastepile. To win the game, not only the pyramid but also the wastepile must be cleared away and discarded.

**Competitive Scoring**—This is a method of playing Pyramid against "par" or another player. A match is six games. In each game two redeals are permitted. If the player clears away the pyramid on the first deal, he scores fifty less the number of cards remaining in the hand, and he may use the redeals to deplete this number. If the pyramid is cleared away in the second deal, the score is thirty-five, less residue of the hand after the third deal. If the pyramid is cleared away in the third deal, the score is twenty less the cards in hand. If the pyramid is not cleared away in three deals, the score is minus the total of cards left in pyramid and hand.

Par is a net score of zero in six games, and any net plus may be considered a win. Two or more players in competition compare their net scores for a series of six games.

Since the order of the cards in hand is known after the first deal, there is scope for some planning of the play in the redeals.

# NESTOR

**(Matrimony)**

The layout in this game is simple but spectacular, and play is uncomplicated.

**Layout**—Deal six rows of eight cards each, with rows overlapping. Do not place two cards of the same rank in the same column. When a card is turned from the pack, and a card of the same rank already lies in the column to which the next card must be dealt, place the card on the bottom of the pack.

The tableau uses all the cards but four. Place these four face down in a pile to form the stock.

**Play**—The bottom card of each column of the tableau is available. Remove available cards by pairs in rank, regardless of suit, and discard.

When play is blocked, turn up top card of the stock. Use it if you can, otherwise discard it and turn up the next stock card. The game is won if entire tableau is discarded by pairs.

# MONTE CARLO

## (Weddings, Double and Quits)

The shifting tableau makes a kaleidoscopic game, with some opportunity for skill.

**Layout**—Deal five rows of five cards each, making a rectangular tableau.

*Layout for Monte Carlo*

**Play**—Two cards of the same rank may be removed from the tableau if they are adjacent vertically, horizontally, or diagonally. (In the diagram, pairs which may be removed are 5's, kings, aces, 10's.) All are discarded.

After all possible pairs are removed, remaining cards must be consolidated. Back them up, preserving order in which they were dealt, until tableau rows are solid from the top down. In the diagram, after removal of four pairs including ♠10 with ♥10, the consolidation will make the second row: ♠8, ♦2, ♠Q, ♣7 ♥J. If you tend to make errors in backing up, pick up the cards in the same order as dealt, left to right, and from top row down, then deal them again in solid rows of five.

After consolidating, deal additional cards in regular order to fill out the tableau to five rows of five. Again remove adjacent pairs. Continue in the same way. The game is won if the entire pack is discarded by pairs.

**Helpful Hints**—With choice of pairing, visualize the adjacencies that will result from the consolidation. In the diagram, pairing ♠10 with ♥10 instead of the ♣10, brings the ♥J adjacent to the ♦J.

# DECADE

This is a difficult game, and you may consider yourself lucky if you have ten cards or less left at the end.

**Layout**—Deal cards in a row singly, face up.

**Play**—Discard any three adjacent cards that add to ten, twenty, or thirty. Count jacks, queens, kings as ten each.

The game is won if all cards but one are discarded.

# BETROTHAL

**(Royal Marriage, Matrimony)**

This marriage is rarely consummated. You may consider it a victory to bring the principals within eight cards of each other.

**Layout**—Place ♥Q on the table at left and place ♥K on bottom of the pack.

**Play**—Deal cards in a row to right of the queen. Whenever two cards of the same suit or same rank are separated by one or two cards in this tableau, throw out the intervening cards. The game is won if, after the entire pack is dealt out, ♥K and ♥Q are side by side, other cards having been discarded.

# ACCORDION

**(Idle Year)**

The best and certainly the most popular game of the family that includes **Decade** and **Betrothal.** Some devotees have compiled records showing chances of winning to be about one in a hundred.

**Layout**—Deal cards in a row. Whenever a card is of the same suit or same rank as the next at its left, or the third at its left, the right-hand card (or pile) may be moved upon the other. If a card matches both the next and the third-next cards, the player may make either move. After each move, look to see if others are now possible. In the diagram, the ♥4 may be moved upon the ♥10. Then this pile may be moved upon the ♣4. The ♥Q may be put upon this pile, and the whole moved upon the ♠Q. Play could have started by moving the ♥4 on the ♥Q, but then the only additional move would have been to put this pile on the ♣4.

Game is won if the entire pack is consolidated in one pile.

*Layout for Accordion*

# GOLF

While making no great demands, Golf offers some scope for skill. It is a favorite for competitive play.

**Layout**—Deal five rows of seven cards each, overlapping. Deal one card below this tableau to start the wastepile.

**Play**—Bottom cards of the tableau columns are available. Object is to clear away tableau by building all the cards upon the waste-pile. Building is in sequence, up or down, regardless of suit. Sequence of rank is not circular. Only a two may be built on an ace, and nothing may be built on a king.

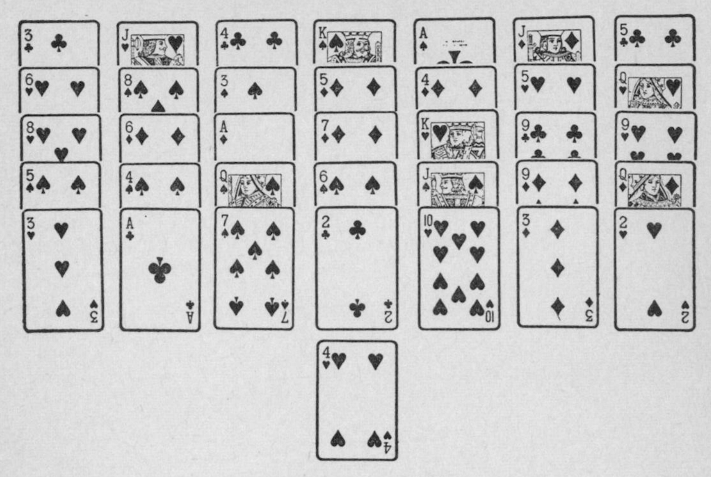

*Layout for Golf*

(In the diagram, the following may be built on the ♥4: ♦3, ♥2, ♣A, ♣2, ♥3, ♠4, ♠5, ♠6, ♦7, ♥8, ♦9, ♥10, ♠J, ♠Q, ♥K. The king stops the sequence.)

Turn up cards from hand singly and place them on the wastepile, using each to take off as many cards from the tableau as possible or expedient. The game is won if the entire tableau is cleared away.

**Competitive Play**—One game of Golf is treated as a "hole." The number of "strokes" taken by the player to make this hole is the number of cards left in the tableau after play is blocked. A hole may be made in zero or less than zero: if the game is won, the number of undealt cards remaining in the hand is a minus score.

One player may compete against "par." Play nine holes and total the scores. You beat par if your total is thirty-six or less.

Two players may compete for lowest total over nine or eighteen holes, or combine "medal" and "match" play. Allow three points for low total over nine holes. Compare scores made on each hole, allowing one point to the winner of each. Thus a player may have one or two bad holes, losing the medal points, and still tie or win the match by winning six or more of the holes.

Three or more players may compete for low total over nine holes. Another plan is to play hole by hole, allowing one point to the winner of each, or a half-point to each of two tying winners. The player who collects three match points first, wins.

# HIT OR MISS

**(Treize, Roll Call, Talkative, Harvest)**

Many a student of card probabilities has been attracted to the problem of determining the chance of winning this game. Don't tackle it unless you have a passion for laborious computation! Empirical methods indicate that the chance of missing completely on going through a complete pack is very slight, but the chance of winning the game is equally slight. You have done well if you reduce the pack to ten cards or less.

Deal cards face up singly into one pile. Count the cards from one to thirteen, then repeat. A card is "hit" if it is of same rank as the ordinal number called. Jack ranks eleven, queen twelve, king thirteen. Discard all cards that are hit. Do not alter the sequence of counting because of a hit. For example, if a 6 is hit, count the next card "seven."

Each time the hand is exhausted, pick up the pile of unhit cards, redeal, and continue the count from where it was stopped. If pack is gone through twice in succession without a hit, the game is lost. To win, every card in the pack must be hit.

# IDIOT'S DELIGHT

**(Aces Up)**

The attraction of this solitaire is that percentage of wins is higher than in most of the other tableau-depleting games.

Aces rank high, above the kings.

**Layout**—Deal four cards in a row.

**Play**—Discard any card lower than another card of the same suit. Continue in the same way, dealing in rows of four upon four fixed piles or spaces, and discarding whenever possible.

A space in the tableau, by removal of an entire pile, may be filled by the top card from any other pile. Of course, the selection should be made if possible so as to release additional cards for discard. Spaces must be filled before a new row of four cards is dealt, if there are enough cards in the tableau for this purpose.

Since aces are high, they may be moved only into spaces. The game is won if, after the entire pack is dealt, only the four aces remain in the tableau, the rest having been discarded.

# ROYAL FLUSH

No choice, hence no skill in this game, which comes out with reasonable frequency.

The royal flush comprises an ace, king, queen, jack, 10 of the same suit.

**Layout**—Deal entire pack into five piles face down (two extra cards on the first two piles).

**Play**—Turn the first pile face up. If the top card is a 10 or higher, it fixes the suit of the royal flush. If not, remove cards one at a time from this pile until you come to a 10 or higher card. If there is none in the first pile, turn up the second and continue the search in the same way.

Having fixed suit of the royal flush, turn up each pile and discard cards from the top until a card of the flush appears. If there is none, the entire pile is discarded. Eventually each of the remaining cards will be topped by a card of the flush.

Pick up the piles in reverse order, so that the last dealt will be at the top of the new hand. Deal all the cards into four piles face down as far as they go. Turn up the piles and discard cards from the top until one of the flush cards appears.

Continue in the same way, discarding cards that cover the uppermost flush card in each pile. Reduce by one the number of piles dealt each time. The game is won if, when only one pile remains, it comprises the five cards of the royal flush and no other.

# PERPETUAL MOTION

**(Idiot's Delight)**

A single game may take from five minutes to five hours. While this characteristic does not endear the solitaire to many, it has its uses. Perpetual Motion is ideal for a long journey when the leisure to play is intermittent. After each session, gather the pack, snap a rubber band around it, put it in your pocket—and next time you can continue from where you left off.

**Layout**—Deal four cards in a row. If two or more are of the same rank, move the others upon the one at the left.

**Play**—Continue dealing the whole pack by rows of four upon the previous piles and spaces. Move cards from right to left whenever they can be matched by rank. These moves are made only with individual cards, not with piles.

When the hand is exhausted, pick up piles in the same order as dealt, turn them over to form a new hand, and deal again by fours.
Whenever four cards of the same rank appear in a row, one at the top of each pile, discard them from the pack. The game is won if all thirteen fours of a kind are so discarded. Continue redealing the pack without limit until the game is won or reaches an impasse. When only twelve or eight cards are left, note the order of the cards before dealing and examine the pack before each subsequent deal to see if this same order has recurred. Once an order recurs identically, the game is blocked.

# CLOCK

### (Travelers, Hidden Cards, Four of a Kind)

While purely mechanical, Clock has the merit of moving fast; you are not kept long in suspense as to the outcome.

**Layout**—Deal thirteen piles of four cards each, face down. Any method of dealing is permitted; simplest is to count off four cards

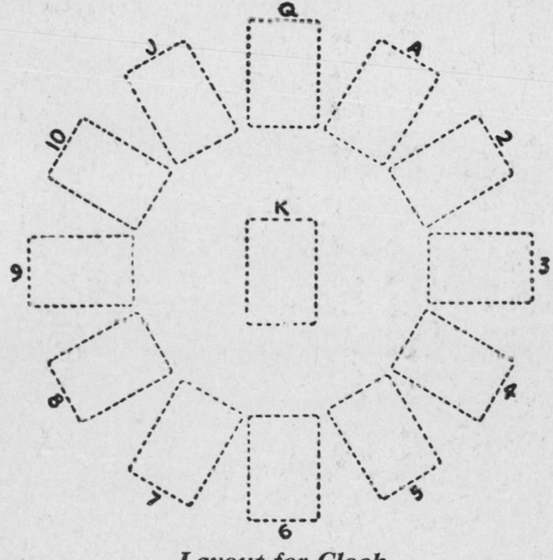


*Layout for Clock*

at a time from the top of the pack. Place twelve of the piles in a circle, representing the numbers on a clock. Put the thirteenth pile in the center. (See diagram.)

**Play**—Turn up the top card of the thirteenth or king pile. Place this card face up underneath the pile of its number. For example, if the card is a queen, put it under the pile in the position of twelve o'clock. If it is a jack, put it under the pile for eleven o'clock, and so on.

Having put a card face up underneath a pile, turn up top card of that same pile and continue play. Should a card turn up on the pile of its own number, as a 6 on the pile at six o'clock, simply put it under and turn up the next card. If there is no next card—the pile now comprising all four cards of the pile number—take instead the top card of the next higher pile. Turn of the fourth king stops the play.

The game is won if all thirteen piles are changed to the proper fours of a kind. If the fourth king is turned up while any cards remain face down, the game is blocked.

# EIGHT-DAY CLOCK

**(Perpetual Motion)**

As the name implies, this game is a more protracted way than simple Clock of finding out whether the pack happened to be shuffled into a favorable order.

**Layout**—Deal thirteen piles of four, arranged as for Clock, but with all cards face up. (See diagram, page 15.)

**Play**—Begin with the first pile, from one up, whose top card is not the same as its number. Thus, if the top of pile one is not an ace, begin there. Lift off the top card and put it under the next pile. Move the top card from that pile to the next, and so on. Go clockwise around the circle of piles, but include pile thirteen after twelve and before one.

In making these transfers, however, skip any pile whose top card is the same as its number. The progressive changes will gradually increase the number of such piles and decrease those remaining in the cycle of shifts. If all the piles become topped with cards of their own number, stop and discard all these thirteen top cards.

The last card removed before such a discard must be held in abeyance. Resume play by putting it under the pile of its own number, or the first thereafter that is not topped by a card of the same number as the pile.

The game is won if three sequences of ace to king are discarded.

A block will result if at any time the circuit of "live" piles does not contain all the cards necessary to complete a sequence. For example, suppose that the transfers have become narrowed down to a circuit of three piles, the two, seven, and twelve piles. Spread these piles for examination. If together they cannot furnish a deuce, a seven and a queen, further play is useless.

# AULD LANG SYNE

This is a simple and very ancient pastime, but fascinating none the less.

**Layout**—Remove the four aces from the pack and place them in a row. These foundations are to be built in sequence up to kings, regardless of suits.

**Play**—Deal a row of four cards below the foundations, forming the reserve. Top cards of reserve piles are available for play on foundations. Spaces in the reserve are not filled except by the deal. Continue to deal in groups of four cards, one on each pile or space. Pause between deals to play up what you can.

*Layout for Auld Lang Syne*

# TAM O' SHANTER

For hardy souls who don't care if they ever win. Follow the rules of Auld Lang Syne except: do not remove the aces from the pack; put them in the foundation row as they become available.

# SIR TOMMY

**(Old Patience, Try Again)**

A derivative of Auld Lang Syne, with the very vital difference of a choice in placing cards from the hand.

**Foundations**—The four aces, as they become available, are to be placed in a row and built up to kings, regardless of suits.

**Play**—Deal four cards, one by one, placing each on any of four wastepiles below the foundations. Play up what you can. Continue dealing cards one by one and placing them as desired on the four piles. Pause to play up to the foundations only after each group of four cards has been placed. Top cards of wastepiles are available for play on foundations. As many or as few cards may be placed on one pile as desired.

# PUSS IN CORNER

So-called because the wastepiles are traditionally placed outside the corner of the foundations, which are placed in a rectangle.

**Foundations**—Remove the four aces from the pack and place them in a row. Each is to be built up to the king in its own color as between red and black.

**Play**—Follow the rules of play for Sir Tommy.

**Redeal**—One redeal is permitted. After the hand is exhausted and play is at a standstill, pick up the four wastepiles in the same order they were dealt, turn them face down, and deal again.

# CALCULATION

Calculation stands at the top of the list of games that give opportunity for skill. Some devotees go so far as to say that two games out of three can be won by patience and application. While this may be an exaggeration, certainly the experienced player wins four or five times as often as the beginner.

**Foundations**—Remove from the pack any ace, deuce, 3, and 4, regardless of suits. Place these four cards in a row to form the foundations. Each is to be built up in arithmetical series as follows, without regard to suits:

A, 2, 3, 4, 5, 6, 7, 8, 9, 10, J, Q, K.
2, 4, 6, 8, 10, Q, A, 3, 5, 7, 9, J, K.
3, 6, 9, Q, 2, 5, 8, J, A, 4, 7, 10, K.
4, 8, Q, 3, 7, J, 2, 6, 10, A, 5, 9, K.

**Play**—Turn up cards from the hand singly and place unplayable cards on any of four wastepiles below the foundations. These piles should be spread downward so that all cards can be read. The top card of each wastepile, as well as the card in hand, is available for play on foundations.

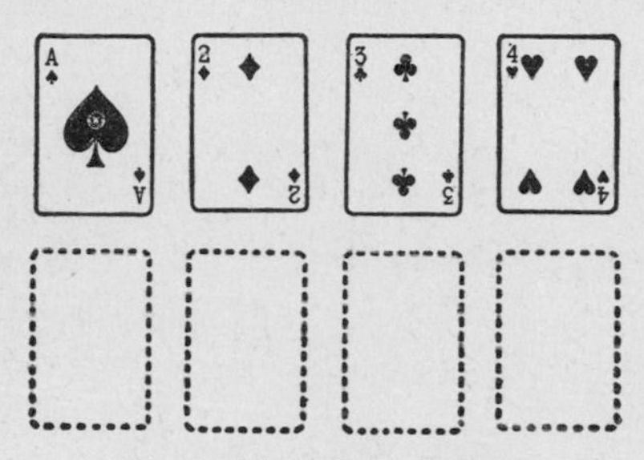

*Layout for Calculation*

# FOUR KINGS

**(Betsy Ross)**

A way of playing Calculation so as to remove most of the choice—hence, most of the opportunity for skill.

*Layout for Four Kings*

**Layout**—Place in a row any ace, deuce, 3, and 4, regardless of suits. These are index cards. In a row below them place any deuce, 4, 6, and 8, regardless of suits. These are foundations.

The foundations are to be built up in arithmetical series. (See Calculation, page 18.) The separate index row serves as a reminder of the arithmetical difference in each series.

**Play**—Turn up cards singly, placing unplayable cards face up on a single wastepile. The top card of this pile, and the card in hand, are available for play on foundations.

**Redeal**—Two redeals are permitted.

# DOUBLE OR QUITS

An oddity among solitaires—there is only one foundation.

**Layout**—Deal two columns of three cards each, then a card between the columns at the top. These seven cards form the reserve. Deal a card between the columns at the bottom, for a foundation. (See diagram.)

**Foundation**—The entire pack exclusive of kings and regardless of suit is to be built on the foundation card in the following circular sequence: A, 2, 4, 8, 3, 6, Q, J, 9, 5, 10, 7, A, etc. Observe that this

*Layout for Double or Quits*

is a doubling sequence. Each card is twice its predecessor, with thirteen subtracted whenever the product exceeds thirteen.

**Play**—If any kings are dealt in the reserve, remove them to the bottom of the pack and deal additional cards to replace them. But if a king is moved into the reserve at any later stage, it must stay there. Kings are dead cards.

All cards in the reserve are available for play on the foundation. In the diagram, on the ♣J may be added: ♥9, ♠5, ♦10, ♣7, ♠A. Spaces in the reserve must be filled from the wastepile, if any, or from the hand.

**Wastepile**—Turn up cards from the hand one by one, placing unplayable cards face up on a single wastepile. The top card of this pile, as well as the card in hand, is available for play on the foundation.

**Redeal**—Two redeals are permitted.

# CARPET

With twenty cards simultaneously available, you should have little difficulty winning this simple game.

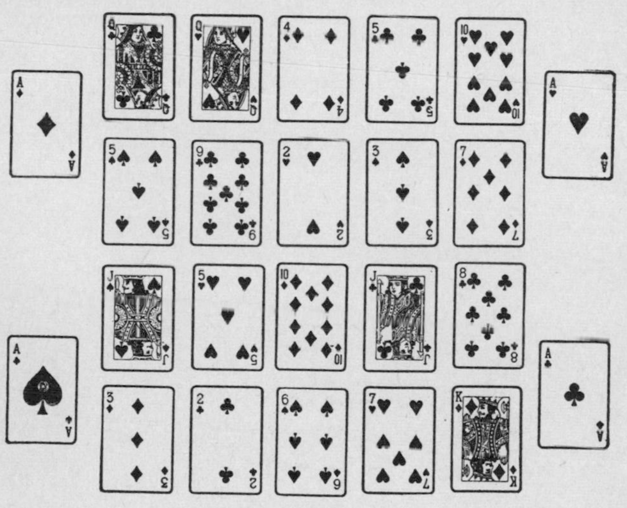

*Layout for Carpet*

**Foundations**—Remove the four aces from the pack and place them in two columns wide apart. The aces are to be built up in suit to kings.

**Layout**—Between the aces deal four rows of five cards each, forming the carpet. (See diagram.)

**Play**—All cards in the carpet are available for play on foundations. Turn up cards from the hand singly, placing unplayable cards face up on a single wastepile. The top card of this pile, as well as the card in hand, is available for play on foundations. Fill spaces in the carpet from the wastepile or from the hand.

# QUADRILLE

### (Captive Queens)

An old-style pictorial solitaire with plenty of action.

**Foundations**—The 5's and 6's, as they become available, are to be moved into a circle. (See diagram.) The 6's are to be built up in

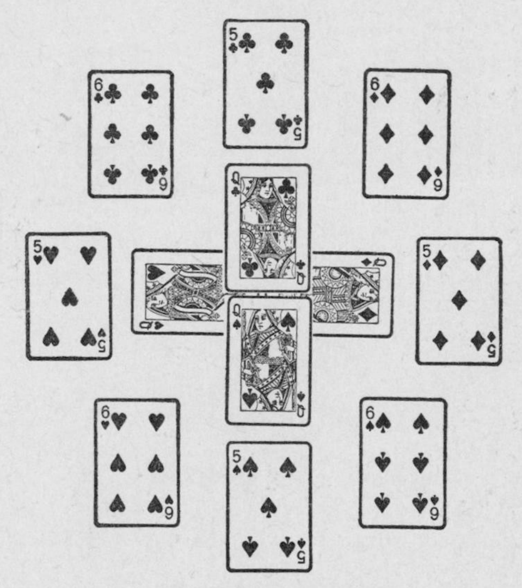

*Layout for Quadrille*

suit to jacks, and the 5's are to be built down in suits to kings, coming after aces.

The queens, as they become available, are to be placed in the center of the circle. These cards are dead, as they are used merely to complete the layout picture.

**Play**—Turn cards up from the pack singly, placing unplayable cards face up on a single wastepile. The top card of this pile, as well as the card in hand, is available for play on foundations.

**Redeal**—Two redeals are permitted.

# THIRTEEN DOWN

## (Eagle Wing)

The face-down stock is found in very few solitaires, though face-down cards on the tableau are common.

**Layout**—Count off thirteen cards face down, and leave them face down in a pile to form the stock. Deal a row of four cards to left of the stock and four more to the right, forming the wings of the reserve. Deal one card above the stock, as the first foundation. (See diagram.)

**Foundations**—The other three cards of same rank as the first foundation are to be moved into a row with it as they become available. The foundations are to be built up in suit until each pile is thirteen cards.

**Play**—Reserve cards are available for play on foundations. Each space in the wings must at once be filled by the top card of the stock, turned face up. After twelve cards have been played off the stock, the thirteenth may be turned face up, and it then is available for

*Layout for Thirteen Down*

play on a foundation as well as into a space. After the stock is exhausted, reserve spaces may be filled from the hand or wastepile, as the player chooses.

**Wastepile**—Turn up cards from the hand one by one, placing unplayable cards face up on a single wastepile. The top of this pile, as well as the card in hand, is available for play on foundations.

**Redeals**—Two redeals are permitted.

# QUEEN'S AUDIENCE

**(King's Audience)**

A simple game that can be won three times out of four.

**Layout**—Deal sixteen cards in the form of a square. This is the antechamber (reserve). The enclosed area is the audience chamber. (See diagram.)

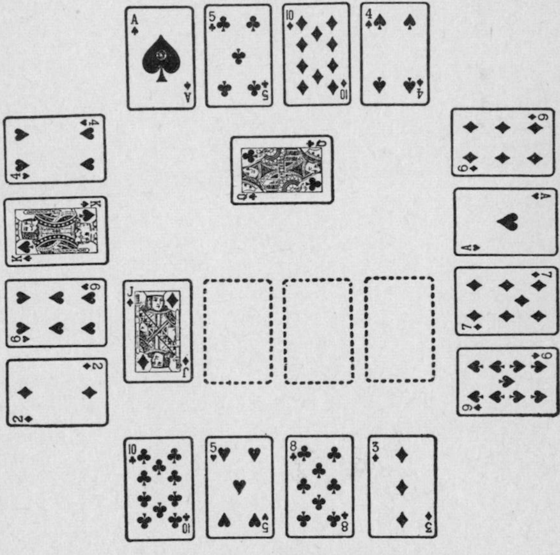

*Layout for Queen's Audience*

**Foundations**—The four jacks are to be moved into the audience chamber as soon as possible and then built down in suit to deuces.

An available jack may be moved in, however, only if the ace of the same suit is also available. The two cards are placed in a pile, jack uppermost, and the ace is thus discarded.

The kings and queens are similarly discarded, but they may be removed only in couples of the same suit as they become available. Pile all the kings and queens together in the audience chamber, keeping a queen uppermost.

**Play**—All cards in the antechamber are available for play on foundations. Turn up cards from the hand singly, filling each space in the antechamber at once and placing unplayable cards face up in a single wastepile. The top card of this pile, as well as the card in hand, is available for play on foundations.

The ace-jack and king-queen couples may be moved into the audience chamber whenever the two cards of a suit are simultaneously available in the antechamber, on top of wastepile, or a card turned from the hand.

# OSMOSIS

## (Treasure Trove)

Several uncommon principles are combined in this game, but they do not avert the common experience of discovering a block in the dregs of the treasure piles. Perhaps you will wish to allow yourself a draw, as in La Belle Lucie.

**Layout**—Count out four stockpiles of four cards each, taking them off the pack face down and squaring them up before turning them over. Place the piles in a column at the left. Deal one card to right of the uppermost stock, forming the first foundation. (See diagram.)

**Foundations**—The three other cards of same rank as the first foundation are to be moved into the column with it as they become available. These cards must be placed in order as they appear, from top to bottom of the column.

All the rest of the cards are to be assembled on the foundations, each card on the foundation of its own suit, but not in order. The cards are best placed in rows, each card overlapping the previous card, so that all can be read.

**Play**—Top cards of stocks are available for play on foundations. Any available card of the suit, from stock or wastepile, may be built on the first foundation. No other suit may be played up until its foundation is in place, and then no card may be played unless another card of the same rank already lies on the foundation row above. For example, if the first foundation is the ♠5, all available

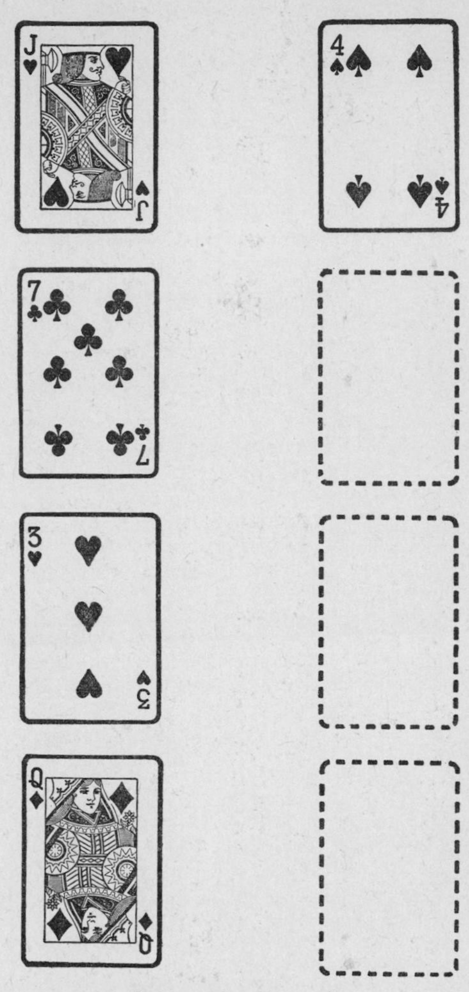

*Layout for Osmosis*

spades may be played up. If the ♥5 is the next foundation, then such hearts may be played up as are paired in rank by spades in the top row.

**Wastepile**—Turn cards up from the hand in groups of three, counted off without changing the order within the group. Place each group face up on a single wastepile. The top card of this pile is available.

**Redeal**—Redealing may continue without limit until the game is won or comes to a standstill.

# KLONDIKE

**(Fascination, Triangle, Chinaman; incorrectly called Canfield)**

It is perhaps a tribute to the indomitable human spirit that this most popular of all solitaires is at the same time one of the most difficult to win.

**Layout**—Deal a row of seven cards, the first face up and the rest face down. Deal a row of six cards upon the first, beginning with one card face up on the second pile and then the rest face down on the piles to the right. Continue with successive rows of five, four, three, two, and one, beginning each time with one card face up, on the pile to the right of that on which the previous row was begun. The completed tableau comprises seven piles increasing in number from one to seven cards, with the top card of each pile face up and the rest face down. (See diagram.)

*Layout for Klondike*

**Foundations**—The four aces, as they become available, are to be moved into a row above the tableau and built up in suit to kings.

**Tableau**—The face-up cards on the tableau may be built down in alternating colors. In the diagram, the ♣10 may be moved upon the ♥J, and the ♦9 upon the ♣10. The ♣3 may be moved upon the ♦4, making a space. Tableau cards may be built on each other, but all face-up cards on a pile must be moved as a unit.

Whenever such a transfer is made, the exposed face-down card on one pile is turned up and becomes available.

Top cards of tableau piles are always available for play on foundations. Aces must be moved up as soon as available, but any higher card may be kept on the tableau for building purposes, if the player wishes, rather than built on a foundation.

A space in the tableau, by removal of an entire pile, may be filled only by a king, or by a build with a king at the bottom.

**Wastepile**—Turn up cards from the hand one by one, placing unplayable cards face up on a single wastepile. The top of this pile, as well as the card in hand, is available for play on foundations or tableau.

# AGNES

One of many variations of Klondike designed to increase the chances of winning.

Follow the rules of Klondike except: after dealing the tableau, deal the next card above it to form the first foundation. The other three cards of same rank are to be moved beside it as they become available. Build foundations up in suit until each pile is thirteen cards. For example, if the foundation is an 8, build: 8, 9, 10, J, Q, K, A, 2, 3, 4, 5, 6, 7. Below the tableau deal a row of seven cards, forming the reserve. All reserve cards are available for play on foundations or tableau. Do not fill spaces in the reserve, except by subsequent deals. Deal a second and then a third row of seven cards upon the piles and spaces of the reserve, pausing each time to make what plays you can. Only the top card of each reserve pile is available. After the third such deal, turn the last two cards of the pack face up, separate from the reserve. These two cards are also available.

# THUMB AND POUCH

When "the Chinaman" takes all your money at Klondike, you can win it back at Thumb and Pouch.

Follow all the rules of Klondike except: in tableau building, a card can be laid on a next-higher of any suit but its own. Face-up cards may be moved one at a time, in part or in whole. A space may be filled by any available card or group.

# WHITEHEAD

A blend of Klondike and Spiderette, Whitehead is only a little easier to win than either of its very difficult progenitors.

Follow the rules of Klondike except: deal all the cards in the tableau face up. Tableau building is in the same color as between red and black. Any available card or group may be put in a space. Available for removal from one pile to another or into a space is the top card of the pile, together with any or all immediately below it that are in unbroken sequence in the same suit. For example, if the ♥6 is on the ♥7, both may be moved together. But if the ♥6 is on the ♦7, the upper card must be moved alone.

# WESTCLIFF

This game is a blend of Klondike and Forty Thieves, and fairly easy to win.

**Layout**—Deal a row of ten cards face down. Deal a second row

*Layout for Westcliff*

upon the first. Deal a third row face up. (See diagram.) This forms the tableau.

**Foundations**—The four aces, as they become available, are moved to a row above the tableau and built up in suit to kings.

**Tableau**—Available tableau cards may be built down in alternating colors. Any or all face-up cards on a tableau pile may be removed to another pile, if the sequence and alternation is correct. When all face-up cards are removed, the exposed face-down card is turned up and becomes available.

A space in the tableau, by removal of an entire pile, may be filled by any available card or group from tableau, wastepile, or hand. Top cards of tableau piles are available for play on foundations.

**Wastepile**—Turn up cards from the hand singly, placing unplayable cards face up on a single wastepile. The top card of this pile, as well as the card in hand, is available for play on foundations or tableau.

# ACES UP

Another variation of Klondike is easier to win because cards from the hand become available in groups, and fewer cards are buried in the layout.

*Layout for Aces Up*

**Layout**—Deal a row of seven cards face down. Deal a second row face down upon the first. Then deal a row face up on the piles, making twenty-one cards in all.

**Foundations**—The four aces, as they become available, are to be moved to a row above the tableau and built up in suit to kings.

**Tableau**—The face-up cards on the tableau may be built down in alternating colors. The top card of each pile is always available. A group of cards on top of a pile, in correct sequence and alternation, may be moved in whole or in part. If all the face-up cards are removed from a pile, turn up the top face-down card, which then becomes available.

Top cards of the piles are always available for play on foundations. Aces must be moved up as soon as available, but any higher card may be kept on the tableau for building purposes, if the player wishes.

A space in the tableau, by removal of an entire pile, may be filled only by a king, or by a build with a king at the bottom.

**Hand**—Whenever play comes to a standstill, deal seven more cards from the hand, one on each tableau pile. Tableau spaces need not be filled before the deal. The last three cards of the pack go on the first three piles.

# SPIDERETTE

Patterned after the two-pack game Spider, Spiderette is much more difficult to win.

**Layout**—Deal twenty-eight cards in seven piles, in the same manner as for Klondike. (See diagram, page 27.)

**Play**—All building is on tableau piles. Cards may be built down, regardless of suit, sequence ending at the ace. Top cards of tableau piles are always available. A group of cards on top of a pile, in correct sequence and all of the same suit, may be moved in whole or in part. When all of the face-up cards on a pile are removed, turn up the face down card, which then becomes available.

A space, by removal of an entire pile, may be filled by any available card or group.

When all thirteen cards of a suit are assembled in correct sequence on top of a pile, they may be discarded. The game is won if all four suits are so assembled and discarded.

Whenever play comes to a standstill, deal an additional row of seven cards, one on each pile, and resume play. All spaces must be filled before a new row is dealt. The last three cards of the pack are dealt on the first three tableau piles.

# WILL O' THE WISP

The major difficulty of Spiderette lies in the large number of buried cards, twenty-one. Will o' the Wisp reduces this number to fourteen, but earns its name because it is by no means so easy to win as it looks on paper.

Follow all rules of Spiderette except: lay out seven piles of three cards each, two face down and one face up.

# FOUR SEASONS

(Corner Card)

A simple game to understand and play, but difficult to beat.

**Layout**—Deal five cards in the form of a cross, forming the tableau. Deal the next card into one of the corner spaces, as the first foundation. (See diagram, page 33.)

**Foundations**—The other three cards of same rank as the first foundation are to be moved to the other corner spaces as they become available. The foundations are to be built up in suit until each pile is thirteen cards, aces following kings.

**Tableau**—Tableau cards may be built on each other downward, regardless of suit. Only one card at a time may be moved from the top of a pile. Spaces may be filled by available cards from the tableau, wastepile, or hand. Top cards of tableau piles are available for play on foundations.

**Wastepile**—Turn cards up from the hand one by one, placing unplayable cards face up on a single wastepile. The top card of this pile, as well as the card in hand, is available for play on foundations or tableau.

# SIMPLICITY

This variation of Four Seasons was probably invented to give emotional relief to frustrated devotees of Four Seasons.

Follow all rules of Four Seasons except: for the tableau deal two rows of six cards each. Deal the next card in a row above for the first foundation. On the tableau, build down in alternating colors.

*Layout for Four Seasons*

# FORTUNE'S FAVOR

If you want to be sure of winning this game, move whole tableau piles at a time, but the given rules make a better contest.

**Foundations**—Remove the four aces from the pack and put them in a row, to be built up in suit to kings.

*Layout for Fortune's Favor*

**Tableau**—Below the aces deal two rows of six cards each for the tableau. These cards may be built on each other, down in suit, but only one card at a time can be moved in the tableau, and never into a space. Spaces must be filled from the wastepile, if any, or from the hand. Top cards of tableau piles are available for play on foundations.

**Wastepile**—Turn cards up from the hand one by one, placing unplayable cards face up on a single wastepile. The top card of this pile, as well as the card in hand, is available for play on foundations or tableau.

**Redeal**—One redeal is permitted.

# CANFIELD

**(Fascination, Demon; incorrectly called Klondike)**

This solitaire takes its name from a celebrated gaming house at Saratoga Springs, N. Y.

**Layout**—Count off thirteen cards face down from the pack, square them up, and place them face up at the left to form the stock. Deal one card above and to right of the stock for the first foundation. In a row to right of the stock deal four cards, forming the tableau. (See diagram.)

**Foundations**—The other three cards of same rank as the first foundation are to be moved to the row with it as they become

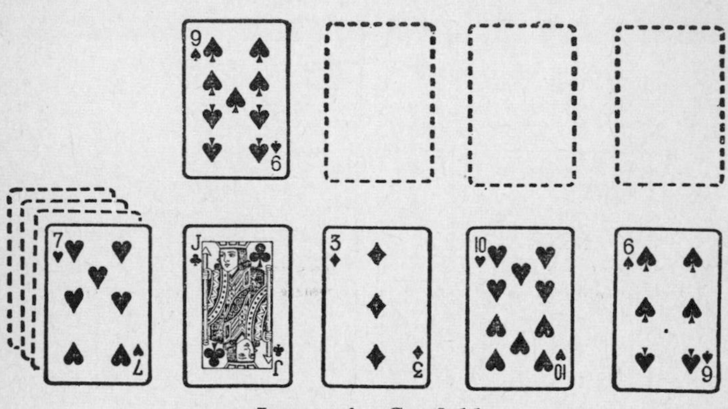

*Layout for Canfield*

available. The foundations are to be built up in suit until each pile is thirteen cards.

**Play**—Tableau cards may be built on each other downward in alternate colors. An entire pile must be moved as a unit in building. (Some players also allow one card at a time to be removed from the top of one pile to another.) Top cards of the piles are available to be played on foundations, but never into spaces.

Spaces must be filled at once from the stock. Top card of the stock also is available to be played on foundations or built on tableau piles. After stock is exhausted, tableau spaces may be filled from wastepile or hand, and the player may keep them open until he wishes to use them.

**Wastepile**—Turn cards up from the hand in groups of three, counted off without altering the order within the group. Place them face up on a single wastepile. The top card of this pile is available for play on foundations or tableau.

Redealing by threes may be continued without limit until the game is won or comes to a standstill.

# SELECTIVE CANFIELD

The object of this variation is to let the player console himself that he **might** have won had he made a correct choice at the outset—if that is any consolation.

Follow all rules of Canfield except: after laying down the stock, deal five cards in a row. Choose one of them for the first foundation. The others remain to form the tableau.

# CHAMELEON

This is a game much like Canfield, even to the degree of difficulty in winning.

**Layout**—Count off twelve cards face down from the pack, square them up, and place them face up at the left to form stock. Deal one card above the stock for the first foundation. In a row to right of the stock deal three cards, forming the tableau. (See diagram.)

**Foundations**—The other three cards of same rank as the first foundation are to be moved to the row with it as they become available. The foundations are to be built up in suit to thirteen cards.

**Play**—Tableau cards may be built on each other downward, regardless of suit. Any or all cards of a pile may be moved as a unit in building. Top cards of tableau piles are available to be played on foundations.

Spaces must be filled at once from the top of the stock. The top card of the stock is available for play on foundations or tableau. After stock is exhausted, the space it occupied becomes a fourth tableau space, and spaces may be filled from hand or wastepile.

**Wastepile**—Turn cards up from the hand one by one, placing unplayable cards face up on a single wastepile. The top card of this pile, as well as the card in hand, is available for play on foundations or tableau.

*Layout for Chameleon*

# STOREHOUSE

**(Thirteen Up, The Reserve)**

A game of the Canfield type that is considerably easier to win.

**Foundations**—Remove the four deuces from the pack and place them in a row, to be built up in suit to aces.

**Layout**—Count off thirteen cards face down from the pack, square them up, and place them face up to left, forming the stock. To right of the stock deal a row of four cards, forming the tableau. (See diagram for Canfield, page 34.)

**Play**—Tableau cards may be built on each other down in suit. An entire pile is moved as a unit in building. Top cards of the piles are available for building foundations.

Spaces must be filled at once from the stock. The top card of the stock is also available for playing on foundations or tableau piles. After the stock is exhausted, spaces may be filled from the hand or wastepile.

**Wastepile**—Turn cards up from the hand one at a time, placing unplayable cards face up on a single wastepile. The top card of this pile, as well as the card in hand, is available for play on foundations or tableau.

**Redeal**—Two redeals are permitted.

# GATE

An interesting tableau-reserve combination, easier to win than might

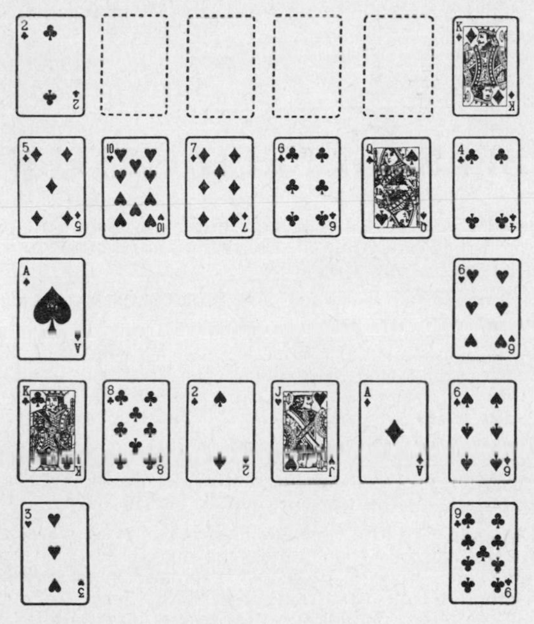

*Layout for Gate*

be thought. It is well to release reserve cards as soon as possible.

**Layout**—Deal two columns of five cards each, forming the posts of the gate (reserve). Between them deal two rows of four cards each, forming the rails (tableau). (See diagram.)

**Foundations**—The four aces, as they become available, are to be moved to a row above the gate and built up in suit to kings.

**Play**—Only the bottom card of each post is available. All cards in the rails are available. These cards (tableau) may be built on each other downward in alternate color. From a rail pile, one card at a time from the top, or the pile as a whole, may be moved to other piles. The top cards are available for play on foundations.

A space in the rails may be filled only from the posts. Available post cards may also be moved to foundations or built on tableau piles.

**Wastepile**—Turn up cards from the hand one at a time, placing unplayable cards face up on a single wastepile. The top card of this pile, as well as the card in hand, is available for play on foundations or tableau.

# BELEAGUERED CASTLE

Beleaguered Castle is one of a large family of games in which the whole pack is laid out. Most of these games are difficult to win, but afford good mental exercise.

**Foundations**—Remove the four aces from the pack and place them in a column, to be built up in suit to kings.

**Layout**—Deal the rest of the pack into two wings of a tableau, one on each side of the foundations. (See diagram.) Each wing is made up of four rows of six cards each, the cards in each row overlapping. The customary method is to deal by columns. First deal a column of four cards far to the left to start the left wing. Then deal a column just to the right of the aces to start the right wing. Continue dealing to the wings alternately, a column at a time, each column overlapping the previous column at the left.

**Play**—Only one card at a time at the open end of each row is available. The open end is that having the uncovered card.

Available cards may be played on foundations, or may be built on each other downward without regard to suit.

A space made by removal of an entire row may be filled by any available card.

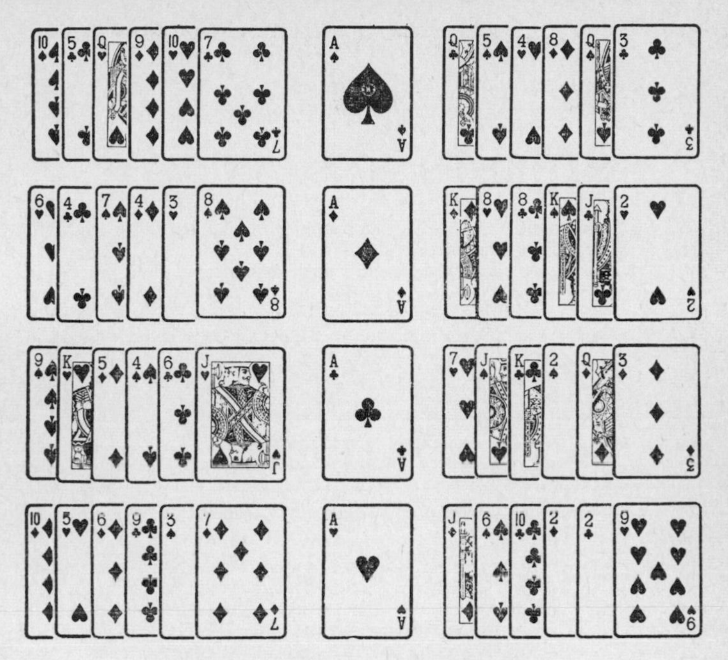

*Layout for Beleaguered Castle*

# CITADEL

This is a variation of Beleaguered Castle which may seem easier to some players. Follow all rules for Beleaguered Castle except: do not place the aces at the outset, but deal them to the center column in the course of laying out the tableau. Any deuce turned up in dealing may be built on its ace already in the center, and so on; a card turned from the pack in dealing may be played to the center, if the foundation is ready for it, but a card once laid on the tableau may not be touched again until the deal is complete. When a card is so played to the center, do not replace it by the next card of the pack, but skip the place in the tableau where it would have gone. The completed tableau rows will thus not be of uniform length.

# STREETS AND ALLEYS

This is Beleaguered Castle made more difficult, but it is unlikely that you will find the parent game too easy.

Follow all rules of Beleaguered Castle except: do not place the aces at the outset; move them into position as they become available. Deal an extra column of cards to the left wing of the tableau, making four rows of seven. (See diagram for Beleaguered Castle, page 39.)

# FORTRESS

This game is perhaps the most popular of those in which the whole pack is laid out.

**Layout**—Deal the entire pack in two wings of a tableau, each wing to consist of five rows with the cards of each row overlapping. The two top rows are six cards, the others, five. The customary method of dealing is by columns. (See diagram, page 41.)

After completing five columns in each wing, place the last two cards on the ends of the two top rows.

**Foundations**—The four aces, as they become available, are to be moved to a column between the wings, to be built up in suit to kings.

**Play**—Only one card at a time may be moved from the open ends of the rows. End cards are available for play on foundations, or to be built on each other in suit, either up or down.

# CHESSBOARD

**(Fives)**

A layout for Fortress too frequently shows no possible move. Such an impasse can usually be circumvented in Chessboard.

Follow rules for Fortress except: after dealing the layout, choose any available card (it may be one made available by building) for the first foundation. The three other cards of the same rank are to be moved to the center as they become available. Build each foundation up in suit until the suit is complete.

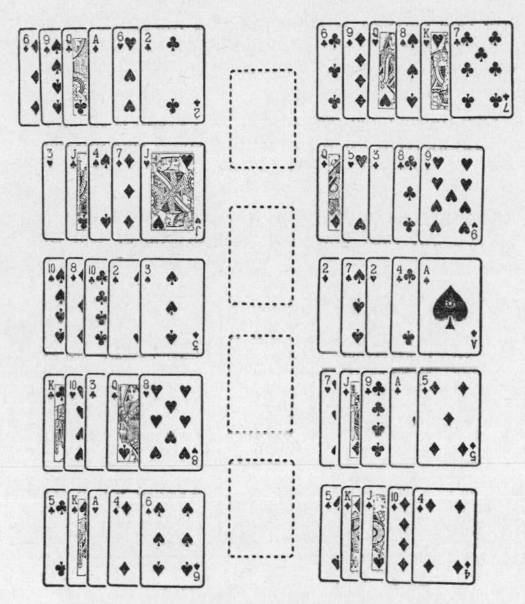

*Layout for Fortress*

# LA BELLE LUCIE

**(Clover Leaf, Midnight Oil, Three Shuffles and a Draw)**

A fascinating game that pays handsome dividends to intelligent planning. Equally absorbing, but much easier to win, are the two-pack variants, House on the Hill and House in the Wood.

**Layout**—Deal the entire pack into seventeen fans of three cards each, with one card left over. (See diagram.) The simplest method of dealing is to count off three cards at a time from the top of the pack and turn them face up, overlapped.

**Foundations**—The four aces, as they become available, are to be placed in a row and built up in suit to kings.

**Play**—Only one card at a time may be moved from the top of a fan. Top cards are available for building on foundations, or building on each other down in suit. A space by removal of an entire fan is never filled.

**Redeal**—Two redeals are permitted. To redeal, pick up all the cards exclusive of foundation piles and shuffle them thoroughly. Then deal again in fans of three, with any one or two odd cards at the end in a separate pile.

**Draw**—After the last redeal, any one card below the top of a fan may be drawn out and used on foundations or fan builds.

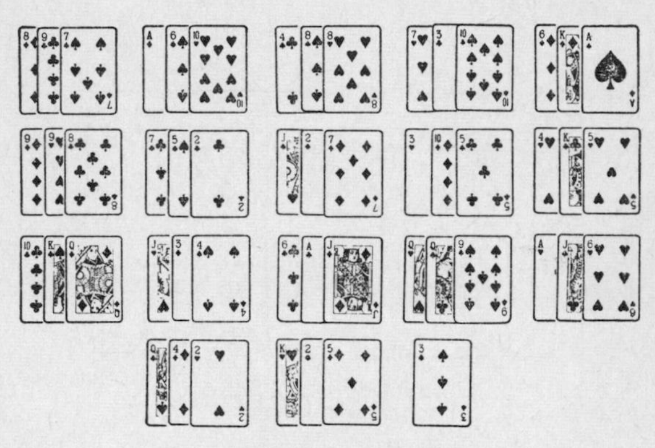

*Layout for La Belle Lucie*

# TREFOIL

This is La Belle Lucie made easier.

Follow all rules of La Belle Lucie except: remove the aces from the pack in advance and place them in a foundation row. The layout then comprises sixteen even fans of three.

# FLOWER GARDEN

## (The Garden)

A solitaire that is neither as easy to win as it looks on paper, nor as difficult as it seems when you first try it.

**Layout**—Deal six rows of six cards each, forming the garden (tableau). Each row should overlap the one above. (See diagram.) Spread the remaining sixteen cards of the pack below the garden to form the bouquet (reserve).

**Foundations**—The four aces, as they become available, are to be moved to a row above the garden and built up in suit to kings.

**Play**—Every card of the bouquet is available for building on foundations or garden piles. The bottom card of each column of the garden is available for building on foundations or on another pile. Garden cards are moved singly and may be built downward, regardless of suit.

A space in the garden, by removal of an entire pile, may be filled by any available card.

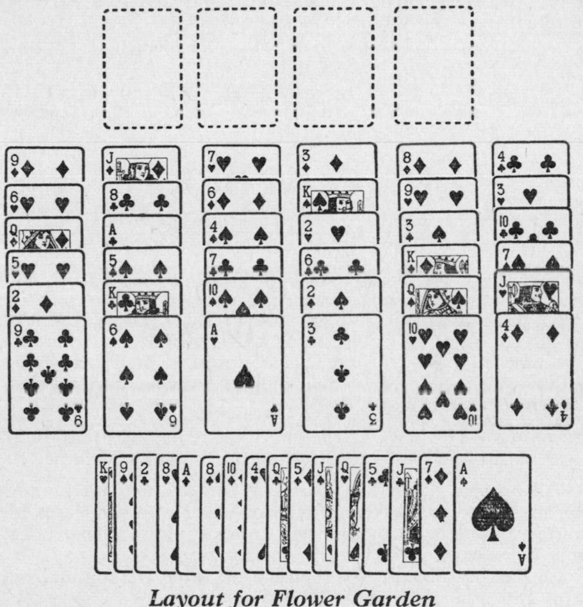

*Layout for Flower Garden*

# SHAMROCKS

This game rivals its cousin, La Belle Lucie, in popularity. In Shamrocks there is more chance that the layout will present no possible move, but also a better possibility of winning if you can get started at all.

**Layout**—Deal the entire pack in seventeen fans of three cards each, with one card left over. (See diagram for La Belle Lucie, page 42.) If any king lies over a lower card of the same suit in the same fan, put it under that card.

**Foundations**—The four aces, as they become available, are to be moved into a foundation row and built up in suit to kings.

**Play**—Only one card at a time may be moved from the top of a fan. Top cards are available for building on foundations. They may also be built on each other downward, regardless of suits, with the proviso that no fan may comprise more than three cards. Thus, the layout is blocked if no ace is on top of a fan and no build can be made on the single card. A space by removal of an entire fan is never filled.

# KING ALBERT

King Albert is a building game of a conventional type.

**Layout**—Deal a row of nine cards. Deal a row of eight overlapping the first, omitting the first card. Add a row of seven, omitting the first two piles at the left. Continue in the same way with rows decreasing by one each time, so as to form nine columns of cards that increase from one to nine. (See diagram.) These forty-five cards form the tableau. Spread the remaining seven cards below the tableau to form the reserve.

**Foundations**—The aces, as they become available, are to be placed in a row above the tableau and built up in suit to kings.

**Play**—All reserve cards are available for building on foundations or tableau. The bottom card of each tableau column is available to be built on foundations or another tableau pile. Tableau piles may be built downward in alternating colors.

A space in the tableau, by removal of an entire column, may be filled by any available card.

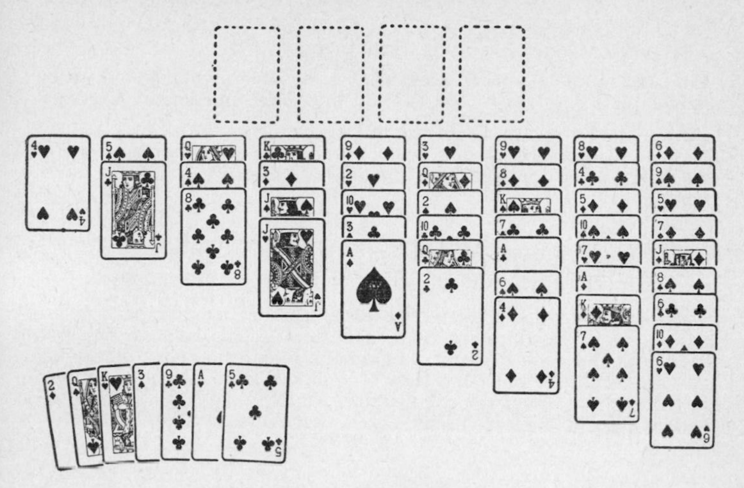

*Layout for King Albert*

# BAKER'S DOZEN

A complex building game in which spaces count nothing and where kings must therefore be treated with deference.

**Layout**—Deal entire pack into four rows of thirteen cards each, with the rows overlapping. (See diagram.) If there is a king in the bottom row, transfer it to the top of its column. If any buried king lies over a lower card of the same suit, move it under that card.

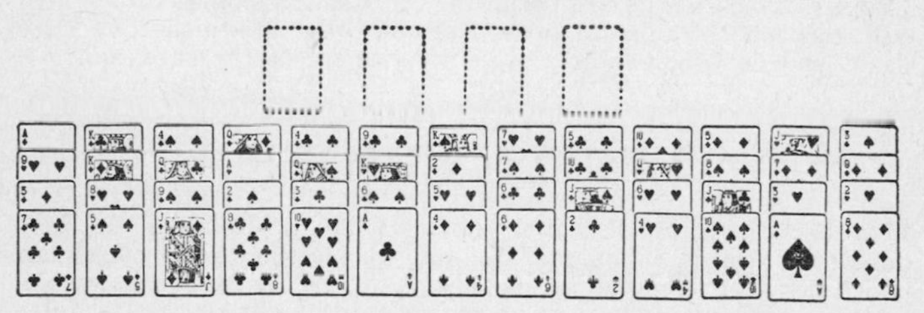

*Layout for Baker's Dozen*

(A simpler rule is to move all kings to the tops of their columns. The game is none too easy, even then.)

**Foundations**—The four aces, as they become available, are to be moved to a row above the tableau and built up in suit to kings.

**Play**—The bottom cards of the tableau columns are available to be played on foundations, and may be built on each other downward, regardless of suit. A space by removal of an entire column is never filled.

# GOOD MEASURE

This is a variant of Baker's Dozen and about as difficult.

Follow all the rules for Baker's Dozen except: remove any two aces from the pack and put them in the foundation row. The other two aces are to be placed as they become available. Deal the tableau in five rows of ten cards each. Before starting play, move all kings to the tops of their columns.

# PERSEVERANCE

This test is a more difficult variant of Baker's Dozen.

**Foundations**—Remove the four aces and place them in a row, to be built in suit up to kings.

**Layout**—Deal the rest of the pack into twelve piles of four cards each. (See diagram for Baker's Dozen, page 45.)

**Play**—The top cards of the piles are available for building on foundations or on each other. On the piles, build down in suit. A group at the top, in correct sequence and suit, may be moved as a unit.

**Redeal**—Two redeals are permitted. When play comes to a standstill, pick up the piles in reverse of the order in which they were dealt, and deal again into twelve piles as far as the cards go.

# LITTLE SPIDER

Don't be discouraged if little opportunity for building develops during the deal in this game. Building during the deal is merely an added privilege. The real business begins when the cards are down—and it is remarkable how business improves under the liberal rules of building.

*Layout for Little Spider*

**Layout**—Deal two rows of four cards each to form the tableau, leaving space between for a row of foundations. (See diagram.) Continue to deal eight cards at a time, one on each pile or space of the tableau. After each eight-card deal, pause and play up what you can as described below. Do not fill spaces in the tableau except in the course of dealing a group of eight cards. The last four cards of the pack are dealt on the upper row.

**Foundations**—Two aces of one color and two kings of the other color, as they become available, are to be moved into a row between the tableau rows. The player has free choice of colors. The foundation aces are to be built up in suit to kings, and the foundation kings are to be built down in suit to aces.

**Play**—The top cards of tableau piles are available. Any available foundation may be moved into place from either tableau row. From the upper row, cards may be played off to all foundations. From the lower row, until the whole pack is dealt, a card may be built only on the foundation directly above the tableau pile.

Once the pack is completely dealt, top cards in the lower row as well as the upper may be played to any foundation, and top tableau cards may be built on each other in sequence up or down, regardless of suit. The sequence is circular, making ace and king adjacent in rank. A space by removal of an entire pile may not be filled.

# GRANDFATHER'S CLOCK

As in the case of the two-pack solitaire, Father Time, this one-pack variant has a pictorial layout.

**Foundations**—Remove from the pack and place in a circle the following twelve cards: ♥2, ♠3, ♦4, ♣5, ♥6, ♠7, ♦8, ♣9, ♥10, ♠J, ♦Q, ♣K. The cards should correspond to the hours on a clock,

*Layout for Grandfather's Clock*

with the nine at twelve o'clock and the rest in sequence. (See diagram.)

Each foundation is to be built up in suit until it reaches the number appropriate to its position in the clock. Sequence is circular (ace after king). The 10, jack, queen, and king foundations will each require four cards, while the rest will require three.

**Layout**—Deal the rest of the pack in five rows of eight cards each, the rows overlapping. This is the tableau.

**Play**—The bottom cards of the tableau columns are available for building on the foundations and may also be built on each other downward, regardless of suit. A space by removal of an entire column may be filled by any available card.

# BISLEY

Bisley is liberal in its rules on foundations, but the uselessness of spaces throws a heavy burden on the player's skill and foresight in building.

**Foundations**—Remove the four aces from the pack and place them in a row at the left. These foundations are to be built up in suit. The four kings, as they become available, are to be moved into a row above the aces and built down in suit. When all the cards of a suit have been built on the ace and king together, the two piles are put together.

**Layout**—Deal nine cards in a row to right of the aces. Deal three more rows of thirteen cards each below the first. (See diagram.) The rows may be dealt overlapping, the aces being pushed up to be clear of the second row of the tableau.

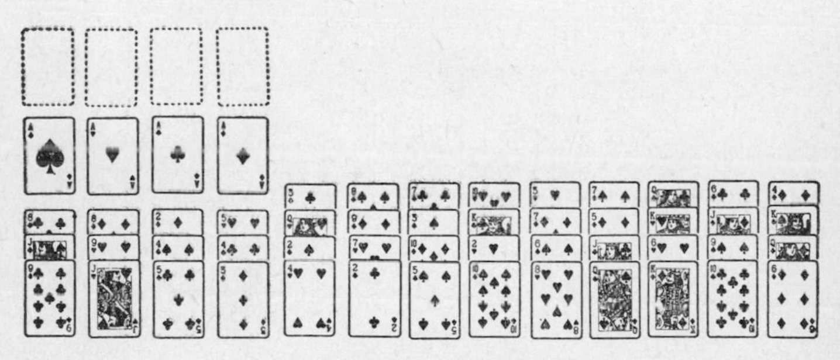

*Layout for Bisley*

**Play**—The bottom cards of the tableau columns are available for play on foundations. They may also be built on each other in suit, up or down. A space by removal of an entire column is never filled.

# PENDULUM

A game whose unique feature is the method of making new cards available.

**Foundations**—Remove the four aces from the pack and place them in a column at the right. These foundations are to be built up in suit by any interval the player chooses after surveying the tableau.

*Layout for Pendulum*

For example, if the choice is to build upward by five, the sequence is: A, 6, J, 3, 8, K, 5, 10, 2, 7, Q, 4, 9. Add the number to the previous card of the series, then subtract thirteen if the sum exceeds thirteen. Whatever interval is chosen must be followed on all four foundations.

**Layout**—Deal the rest of the pack into six rows of eight cards each, all cards separate. (See diagram.)

**Play**—The bottom cards of tableau columns are available to be played on foundations or tableau.

An available card may be placed upon the card just above it in the column, if the upper card is of same suit and next-higher in the chosen sequence. If, for example, the interval is five upward, a ♣3 may be moved upon a ♣8. Should several adjacent cards at the bottom of a pile be in suit and in upward sequence going up the column, all may be stacked on the uppermost card of the sequence.

Any available card, regardless of column, may be moved upon either of the cards at the two upper corners of the tableau, if suit and sequence are correct.

A space by removal of an entire column may be filled only by a card which is last in the chosen sequence. For example, if the interval is five upward, only a 9 may be put in a space. The card goes in the top row of the tableau. Spaces must be filled if possible, but the operation of the pendulum is not altered by a space in the top row.

**The Pendulum**—When play comes to a standstill, "swing the pendulum." The first swing must be to right, and thereafter to left and right alternately. The pendulum consists of moving all cards in rows containing spaces, *except the top row*, to the right or left side of the tableau, without changing the order of cards in the row. The spaces thus being massed toward one lower corner of the tableau, new cards above them become available. The pendulum may be swung without limit until the game is won or becomes blocked.

# GAPS

A purely mechanical exercise, but plenty of action makes this game an agreeable pastime.

**Layout**—Deal the entire pack in four rows of thirteen cards each. Then discard the aces from the layout, creating four spaces or gaps. (See diagram, page 52.)

**Play**—Into each space move the card next-higher in suit to the card at the left of the space. Sequence ends with the king, so that no card may be moved into a space at right of a king. Continue making all possible shifts until blocked because all spaces are at the right of kings.

*Layout for Gaps*

A space at the extreme left of a row may be filled by any deuce. The game is won if all cards are arranged in sequence from deuce up to king, one suit on each row.

**Redeal**—One redeal is permitted. When play is blocked, pick up all the cards not in proper suit and sequence, with deuces at left ends of the rows. Shuffle the cards and deal them so as to fill out each row to thirteen, including one space just to right of the established sequence in the row. Continue play as before. If the game again becomes blocked, it is lost.

# SCORPION

Although largely mechanical, Scorpion is a highly colorful way of finding out if the chance of the deal has created any "crisscrosses." Where none exist, you are bound to win.

**Layout**—Deal a row of seven cards, four face down and three face up. Deal two more rows in the same way upon the first, the cards overlapping. Continue with four more overlapping rows, all cards face up. (See diagram.) The tableau thus comprises forty-nine cards. Place the remaining three cards aside, face down, as the reserve.

**Play**—The card next-lower in suit may be placed upon the bottom card of a tableau column, except that nothing may be built upon an ace. Available for building is any card face up in the tableau, regardless of how deeply buried. Such card, together with all that cover it, may be picked up and moved as a unit.

Whenever all the face-up cards are cleared off one of the first three columns, turn up the top face-down card, which then becomes available.

*Layout for Scorpion*

A space by removal of an entire column may be filled only by a king. Any face-up king is available for this purpose, covering cards being moved with it as a unit.

The game is won if all four suits become assembled in descending sequence upon the kings.

**Reserve**—When play comes to a standstill, deal the three reserve cards, one on the bottom of each of the first three columns. It is not obligatory to fill spaces before dealing the reserve. Continue play until it comes to a standstill, or the game is won.

# YUKON

A blend of two largely mechanical games, Klondike and Scorpion, Yukon affords surprising scope for skillful manipulation.

**Layout**—Deal twenty-eight cards in seven pyramidal piles. (See Klondike, page 27.) Then deal the remaining twenty-four cards in four overlapping rows upon the six piles other than the single card. (See diagram, page 54.)

**Foundations**—The four aces, as they become available, are to be placed in a row above the tableau and built in suit up to kings.

*Layout for Yukon*

**Play**—On the bottom card of a tableau column may be built a card of opposite color and next-lower in rank. Available for building is any card face up in the tableau, regardless of how deeply buried. Such card, together with all that cover it, may be picked up and moved as a unit.

Aces may thus be built on deuces, but not kings on aces. An ace at the bottom of a column must be moved up to the foundation row.

Whenever all the face-up cards are cleared off a pile, turn up the top face-down card, which then becomes available. Bottom cards of all columns are available for play on foundations, but none other than aces need be played up until the player chooses.

A space by removal of an entire column may be filled only by a king. Any face-up king is available for this purpose, covering cards being moved as a unit.

**Helpful Hints**—Get the face-down cards into play as quickly as possible. Play on foundations only to further this end. In building, try to keep foundations abreast in rank. To build one far ahead of the others may deprive the tableau of cards vitally needed for building.

# AMAZONS

The four queens are amazons who top the foundations when the game is won, but you will be lucky if you ever see this finale.

**Pack**—Discard from one pack all the kings, deuces, 3's, 4's, 5's, and 6's. The remaining cards rank normally from queen high down to 7, with aces below the 7's.

**Layout**—Deal four cards in a row to start the reserve.

**Foundations**—The four aces, as they become available, are to be placed in a row above the reserve and built in suit up to queens. The aces must be placed, strictly in the order they appear, from left to right.

**Play**—The top of a reserve pile is available for play on the foundation immediately above it. Do not fill spaces in the reserve except in the course of dealing. Deal cards four at a time, one on each reserve pile, playing up what you can between deals. Continue until the pack is exhausted.

**Redeal**—Two redeals are permitted. To redeal, pick up the four reserve piles in the same order as they were dealt, turn them over to form a new hand, and deal again.

# POKER SOLITAIRE

**(Poker Squares)**

**Layout**—Deal twenty-five cards into a tableau of five rows of five cards each.

**Play**—Place each card to best advantage, so long as it remains within the confines of the tableau. (An alternate rule is that each card must be placed adjacent horizontally, vertically, or diagonally to some card previously dealt.)

Score the five cards in each row and column of the tableau as a poker hand. Two methods of scoring are prevalent, as follows:

| *Hand* | *English* | *American* |
|---|---|---|
| Royal flush | 30 | 100 |
| Straight flush | 30 | 75 |
| Four of a kind | 16 | 50 |
| Full house | 10 | 25 |
| Flush | 5 | 20 |
| Straight | 12 | 15 |
| Three of a kind | 6 | 10 |
| Two pairs | 3 | 5 |
| One pair | 1 | 2 |

The English system takes account of the peculiarities of the solitaire. Trying for a straight is hazardous, as there is likely to be no score at all if it fails; trying for a full house is sure to give a score at least for one or two pairs, or a triplet.

The object is to place the cards so as to make the highest possible total score.

See also Multiple Solitaire, page 128.

# CRIBBAGE SOLITAIRE—I

This game is one to amuse a cribbage player without an opponent.

**Layout**—Deal six cards face down to make the hand, and two face down to start the crib.

**Play**—Look at the hand and lay away two cards to the crib. Turn up the next card of the pack for the starter. Score the hand, then turn up and score the crib. Follow cribbage rules in scoring.

Put the starter on the bottom of the pack and discard the other eight cards. Deal again in the same way. Continue dealing and discarding until only four cards remain in the pack. Turn these up and score them as a hand without a starter.

Object is to make the highest possible total on running once through the pack. By tradition, a score of 120 is considered to be a "win."

# CRIBBAGE SOLITAIRE—II

**(Cribbage Squares)**

This is another game on the cribbage principle, limited, however, by one deal.

**Layout**—Deal sixteen cards one by one in a tableau of four rows of four cards. Each card may be placed to best advantage, with the proviso that it must be adjacent horizontally, vertically, or diagonally to some card previously dealt.

**Play**—Turn the seventeenth card of the pack face up as the starter. Score each row and each column in the tableau as a cribbage hand, together with the starter in every case.

The object is to place the cards as dealt so as to make the highest possible total score. A total of sixty-one or more may be considered a "win."

# CRIBBAGE SOLITAIRE—III

Deal cards one by one in a row, not overlapping. Look for any of the following scoring combinations in two or three adjacent cards:

| | |
|---|---|
| One pair | 2 |
| Three of a kind | 6 |
| Three of same suit | 3 |
| Three in sequence | 3 |
| Three in suit and sequence | 6 |
| Two or three cards totaling 15 | 2 |

Note that as in cribbage, a sequence is valid even though the cards do not lie in sequential order. For example, 7-5-6 is a sequence if the cards are adjacent.

Score each combination, then move any one of the cards involved upon any other. The choice here should be exercised so as to make additional scoring combinations, when possible. For example, with 9-7-5-6 score the sequence, then move the 6 on the 7 and score for the fifteen, 9-6.

A combination must be scored and consolidated at once, before another card is dealt, with the exception that when a pair appears a third card may be dealt, to try for three of a kind.

The object is to make the highest possible total score on running once through the pack. A total of sixty-one or more is a "win."

# JUVENILE SOLITAIRES

## EVEN UP

An excellent juvenile pastime designed to teach addition painlessly.

**Pack**—Discard from one pack all the jacks, queens, and kings.

**Play**—Deal cards one at a time in a single overlapping row. Remove and discard any two adjacent cards whose numerical total is an even number. The game is won if the entire pack is discarded.

## KNOCKOUT

**(Hope Deferred)**

A juvenile game that gives practice in collecting, shuffling, and dealing the cards.

**Pack**—Discard from one pack all deuces, 3's, 4's, 5's, and 6's.

**Play**—Deal three cards in a row, and if any are clubs discard them. Fill spaces at once from the pack. Continue dealing three cards at a time, one on each pile of the layout, and discarding any clubs that appear. Fill a space only when an entire pile is removed. Stop after having dealt five times—a total of fifteen cards plus any dealt to fill spaces.

Gather all the cards exclusive of the clubs discarded, shuffle them thoroughly, and start again. Two such redeals are permitted. The game is won if all the eight clubs are discarded.

## PAIRS

**(The Star)**

This is a game for children who have reached the age when pictorial layouts are worth the trouble.

**Pack**—From one pack discard all deuces, 3's, 4's, 5's, and 6's.

**Layout**—Deal sixteen cards in the form of two concentric circles. Place the rest of the pack face down in the center. (See diagram.)

**Play**—Turn cards one by one from the pile in the center. Each card must be paired with another of the same rank in the tableau, the two cards being discarded. Each space in the tableau is filled at once from the hand.

The first time a card is turned from the center pile that is not paired by a card in the tableau, any two tableau cards that are a pair may be discarded and the spaces filled. But thereafter the game is lost if a second unusable card is turned from the hand.

*Layout for Pairs*

The game is won if the entire hand is turned up and used. The cards then remaining in the tableau may be added in pairs to the discard pile, to complete the picture.

# THE WISH

An ancient belief is that if you win this solitaire your wish of the moment will be granted.

**Pack**—Discard from one pack all the deuces, 3's, 4's, 5's, and 6's.

**Play**—Deal the entire pack into eight piles of four cards each face down. Then turn them all face up, keeping them squared so that only the top cards can be read. Remove and discard cards from the tops of the piles in pairs. The game is won if the entire pack is so discarded.

# TWO-PACK SOLITAIRES

## EIGHTEENS

**(The Wheel, Ferris Wheel)**

This game is a purely mechanical pastime for whiling away idle moments.

**Layout**—Discard all eight aces and deal three rows of four cards each for the tableau.

**Play**—Remove cards from tableau in groups of four, comprised of one face card and three other cards whose numerical total is eighteen. Taking two cards of the same rank in one group (such as two 7's and a 4), is prohibited.

Cards removed from the tableau are discarded and spaces filled from the hand.

Game is won if all cards in the hand are dealt into the tableau.

## VIRGINIA REEL

Look before you build, or a hasty move may block you! Skillful play can win this intricate game as often as once in three times.

**Layout**—Remove a deuce, 3, and 4 of different suits from the pack and place them in a column at the left. To the right of each card deal a row of seven more cards for the tableau Deal another row of eight cards below the tableau, starting the wastepiles. (See diagram, page 62.)

**Foundations**—All deuces, 3's, and 4's are foundations. They must be placed, each in its own row, as shown by the column at the left. The game is won by building foundations in suit and sequence as follows: 2, 5, 8, J; 3, 6, 9, Q; 4, 7, 10, K.

**Play**—No foundation can be built up until it is in its proper row. (In the diagram, the only additional foundation in its proper row is ♣2.)

Foundations dealt in different rows may be exchanged if each is thereby brought into its proper row. Aces are dead cards and may be replaced in tableau as soon as a foundation is available to replace it.

**Available Cards**—Top cards of wastepiles and tableau cards not built on foundations are available, provided that spaces created can be filled immediately. After making all desired plays in the original

*Layout for Virginia Reel*

layout, deal another row of eight cards on the wastepiles, make possible plays, and continue in this fashion until pack is exhausted. A vacancy in a wastepile is not filled except by the next deal of eight cards from the hand.

**Helpful Hints**—Don't swap foundations in the tableau until they are needed for building. Sometimes they can be moved singly to better advantage. Also important to remember is to save foundations from becoming buried in wastepiles.

# ROYAL PARADE

**(Hussars, Three-Up)**

This is the progenitor of Virginia Reel. It is much harder to win, having less scope for maneuver, but therefore is a welcome change when you are not in the mood for deep study.

Follow all rules of Virginia Reel except: discard all eight

aces in advance; do not place a column of foundations at the left; deal three rows of eight cards each for the tableau; and get all the foundations into position by regular play.

# PATRIARCHS

A patriarchal game indeed, a simple building solitaire from which many more complicated games are descended.

**Foundations**—Remove one ace and one king of each suit from the pack. Put the aces in a column at the left, to be built up in suit to kings. Put the kings in a column at the right, to be built down in suit to aces.

**Reserve**—Between the columns of foundations, deal three rows of three cards each, forming the reserve. (See diagram.) All cards of the reserve are available for play on foundations. Spaces must be filled at once from the wastepile, or from the hand.

**Wastepile**—Turn up cards from the hand one by one, placing unplayable cards face up on a single wastepile. The top card of this pile, as well as the card in hand, is available for play on foundations.

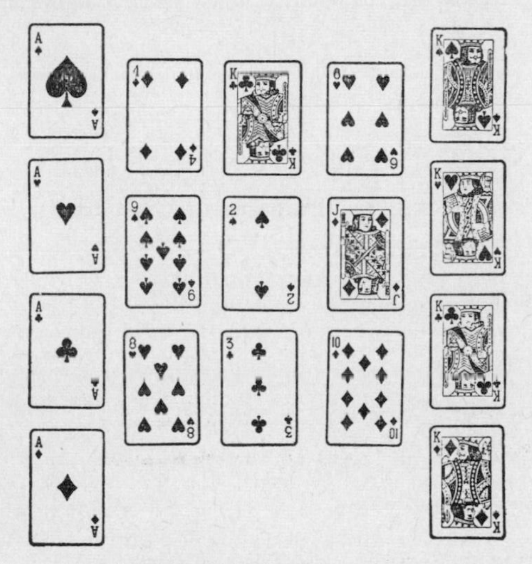

*Layout for Patriarchs*

**Reversal**—When the top cards of the two foundations of the same suit are in sequence, any or all cards of one pile may be reversed upon the other, except for the ace or king at the bottom.

**Redeal**—One redeal is permitted.

# CONTRA-DANCE

**(Cotillion)**

The traditional layout of the sixteen foundations is in a circle, but the game is just as good with the more convenient arrangement here suggested.

**Foundations**—Remove all 6's and 5's from the pack and place them in two rows, the 5's above and the 6's below. The 6's are to be built up in suit to queens; the 5's are to be built down in suit to kings (following after aces).

**Play**—Turn cards from the hand one by one, placing unplayable cards face up on a single wastepile. The top card of this pile, as well as the card in hand, is available for play on foundations.

**Redeal**—One redeal is permitted.

# SULTAN OF TURKEY

**(The Sultan, Emperor of Germany)**

The intended final picture shows the lone monarch surrounded by his harem. Only an exceptional run of cards can deprive you of this elegant view.

**Layout**—Remove the eight kings and one ♥A from the pack. Place them in three rows of three with a ♥K in the center and the ace below it. (See diagram.) These are the foundations. Deal a column of four cards on each side of the foundations, forming the divan or reserve.

**Foundations**—Do not build on the central ♥K. All other kings are to be built up in suit to queens. The ♥A is to be built up in suit to the queen.

**Play**—All cards of the divan are available for play on foundations. A space in the divan must be filled at once from the wastepile, if any, or hand.

*Layout for Sultan of Turkey*

**Wastepile**—Turn cards from the hand one by one, placing unplayable cards face up on a single wastepile. The top card of this pile, as well as the card in hand, is available for play on foundations.

**Redeal**—Two redeals are permitted.

# CRAZY QUILT

### (Quilt, Carpet, Japanese Rug)

The sprawling layout of many pictorial solitaires can be condensed for convenience—but not Crazy Quilt. The huge tableau has a real reason—a unique way of determining the availability of cards.

**Layout**—Remove one ace and one king of each suit from the pack for foundations. Put the aces in a column at the extreme left, and the kings in a column at the extreme right. Between the columns deal sixty-four cards in a "crazy quilt" of eight rows of eight, turning cards alternately. (See diagram, page 66.) This is the tableau.

*Layout for Crazy Quilt*

**Foundations**—The aces are to be built up in suit to kings, and the kings down in suit to aces.

**Play**—A tableau card is available for play on foundations if it has a narrow edge free. At the outset, four cards are available along each side. The removal of a card releases others by leaving a space across their narrow edges. For example, playing the ♥2 from the bottom edge in the diagram will release the ♣9 and ♦7. Game is won if all tableau cards are released and all foundations are built in suit.

Spaces in the tableau are never filled. A prime object is to get into the tableau as quickly as possible in order to get all cards into play.

**Wastepile**—Turn cards up from the hand one at a time, placing unplayable cards face up on a single wastepile. The top card of this pile, as well as the card in hand, is available for play on foundations.

Available tableau cards may be built upon the top card of the wastepile in suit, either up or down. Sequence of rank is circular, so that an ace may be built on a king or vice versa.

**Redeal**—One redeal is permitted.

# WINDMILL

**(Propeller)**

A breezy game that often sails along on air—and as often lets the player down with a thud. Just when you think you have won, you find you have been building a castle in the air.

**Layout**—Place any one ace in the center of the table. Deal two cards in column above it and two in column below; two in a row to left of the ace and two in a row at the right. (See diagram.) These eight cards are the reserve.

**Foundations**—The center ace is to be built up, regardless of suit, until the pile contains fifty-two cards. Sequence is circular. The first four kings of any suits that become available are to be moved into the spaces between the arms of the cross. These four foundations are to be built down to aces, regardless of suit.

*Layout for Windmill*

**Play**—All eight cards of the reserve are available for play on foundations. The top card of a king-foundation may be transferred to the ace-foundation, but only one such card may be moved from a given pile at a time. After such a transfer, the next card built on the ace-foundation must come from the reserve, the wastepile, the hand, or another king-foundation. The king itself also may be moved from a king-foundation to the center pile. Each space in the reserve must be filled at once from the wastepile, if any, or from the hand.

**Wastepile**—Turn up cards from the hand one at a time, placing unplayable cards face up on a single wastepile. The top card of this pile, as well as the card in hand, is available for play on foundations.

# THE FAN

The name is derived from the traditional way of placing the reserve —in a crescent above the rest of the layout. However, in this elaborate building game you may find your hands too full to bother with pictures!

**Layout**—Count off twelve cards face down, square up the pile, and place it face up at the left to form the stock. To right of it deal a row of twelve cards, overlapping, to form the reserve or fan. Below the stock deal one card, the first foundation. The other foundations will go in a row beside the first. Below the space reserved for them, deal a row of four cards, forming the tableau. (See diagram.)

*Layout for The Fan*

**Foundations**—The other seven cards of same rank as the first foundation are to be moved into the foundation row as they become available. All foundations are to be built in sequence, regardless of suits, until each pile contains thirteen cards. The player has the option, after inspecting the reserve, of electing to build up or down. His decision, which may be delayed until the first card is placed on a foundation, applies to all eight piles.

**Play**—Available for play on foundations are the top card of the stock, the top card (right end of the fan) of the reserve, all cards of the tableau, the top card of the wastepile, and cards turned from the hand.

A space in the tableau must be filled from the hand or wastepile.

**Wastepile**—Turn up cards from the hand one at a time, placing unplayable cards face up on a single wastepile.

**Redeal**—Two redeals are permitted.

# PRECEDENCE

**(Order of Precedence, Panama Canal)**

This game usually starts so slowly that it looks hopeless, but often provides pleasant surprises before the end.

**Foundations**—Remove any one king from the pack and place it at the left. In the same row are also to be placed a queen, jack, 10, 9, 8, 7, and 6, regardless of suit, as they become available. These foundations are to be built down, regardless of suits, until each pile consists of thirteen cards. The top cards will then rank in order from ace down to seven.

**Play**—Turn up cards from the hand one by one, placing unplayable cards face up on a single wastepile. The top card of this pile, as well

*Layout for Precedence*

as the card in hand, is available for play on foundations.

Place foundations as quickly as possible in a row with the king, as they become available, but observe the rule that no base card may be placed until all the others of higher rank have been placed. For example, no jack may be moved into the foundation row to start the third pile until a queen has been placed to start the second.

Building on foundations already placed is permissible at all times.

**Redeal**—Two redeals are permitted.

# SALIC LAW

This venerable game, in which the queens are discarded, no doubt took its name from that provision of Frankish law denying daughters the right to inherit land.

**Layout**—Remove one king from the pack and place it at the left. Deal cards face up on this king, overlapping downward in column,

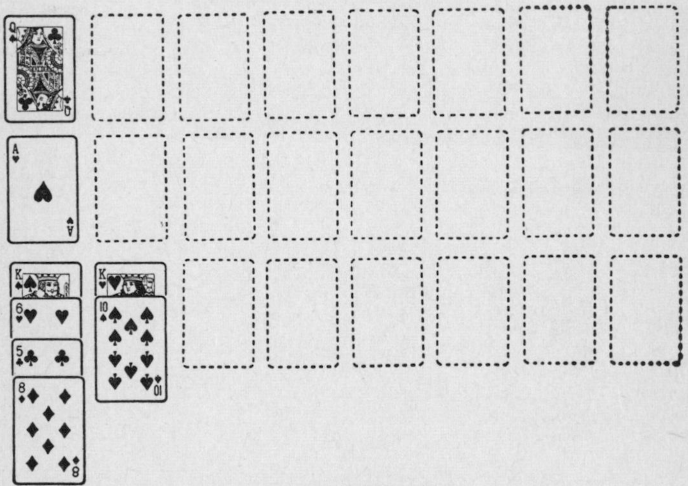

*Layout for Salic Law*

until another king appears. Place the second king at right of the first, and deal cards upon it until the third king appears. Continue in the same way to deal out the whole pack upon the eight kings, which should be arranged in a row. (See diagram.)

During the deal, separate all aces and queens. Place the aces in a row above the kings, and the queens in a row above the aces. (The queen-row is solely for pictorial effect. They can be discarded.)

**Foundations**—Aces are foundations, to be built up, regardless of suit, to jacks.

**Building**—Building on foundations may begin as soon as the first ace is placed. Cards as turned from the hand in dealing are available, together with the top cards of all king-piles (bottom cards of the columns).

If all the cards dealt on a king are played off, the uncovered king is the equivalent of a space. Any available card may be placed on it. But spaces may not be utilized until after the deal is finished. If play on foundations and tableau comes to a standstill at any time after the last card is dealt, the game is lost.

# FAERIE QUEEN

This variant of Salic Law gives somewhat more opportunity for skill.

Follow all rules of Salic Law except: do not discard the queens from the play. The ace-foundations are to be built up to queens. After the deal is finished, available cards may be built on each other downward, regardless of suit.

# INTRIGUE

A variant of Salic Law probably devised by someone who wanted to win every time.

Follow all rules of Salic Law except: use queens for base cards instead of kings. During the deal, throw out 5's and 6's instead of aces and queens. The 6's are to be built up, regardless of suit, to jacks, and the 5's to be built down, regardless of suit, to kings, following after aces.

Some competition can be put into this game by adopting this rule: each queen placed in the base row permits the placing of a

5 and a 6 in column above it. Should a foundation card appear at a time when there is no queen to receive it, it must be dealt on the pile. For a really difficult game, adopt the rule that each foundation card must be put in column above a queen of its own suit. Lacking such a queen in the base row, a foundation must be dealt on a pile.

# ODD AND EVEN

A simple exercise in alternate building in which much depends on how quickly Lady Luck supplies aces and deuces.

**Layout**—Deal three rows of three cards each, forming the reserve.

**Foundations**—One ace and one deuce of each suit, as they become available, are to be placed in a row above the reserve. (See diagram.) The aces are to be built up in suit and skip-sequence: A, 3, 5, 7, 9, J, K, 2, 4, 6, 8, 10, Q. The deuces are to be built up in suit and skip-sequence: 2, 4, 6, 8, 10, Q, A, 3, 5, 7, 9, J, K.

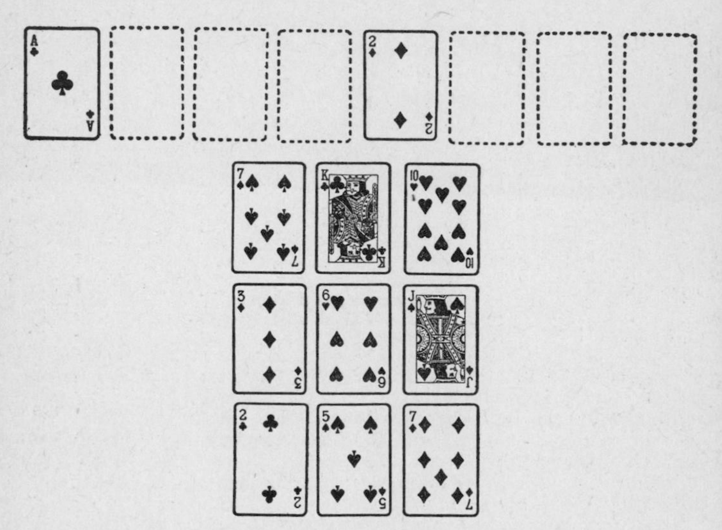

*Layout for Odd and Even*

**Play**—All cards of the reserve are available for play on foundations. A space in the reserve must be filled at once from the wastepile or from the hand.

**Wastepile**—Turn up cards from the hand one at a time, placing unplayable cards face up on a single wastepile. The top card of this pile, as well as the card in hand, is available for play on the foundations.

**Redeal**—One redeal is permitted.

# ROYAL COTILLION

There is a great deal to watch in Royal Cotillion. But then, the more cards available at one time, the better the chances of winning!

**Layout**—At the left, deal three rows of four cards each, forming the left wing of the reserve. At the right, deal four rows of four cards each, forming the right wing. Leave space between the wings for two additional columns of cards. (See diagram.)

**Foundations**—One ace and one deuce of each suit, as they become available, are to be moved to the center. The aces are to be built up in suit and skip sequence: A, 3, 5, 7, 9, J, K, 2, 4, 6, 8, 10, Q. The

*Layout for Royal Cotillion*

deuces are to be built up in suit and skip-sequence: 2, 4, 6, 8, 10, Q, A, 3, 5, 7, 9, J, K.

**Reserve**—Only the bottom card of each column of the left wing is available, and spaces are never filled. All cards of the right wing are available, and each space must be filled at once from the wastepile, if any, or from the hand. Play available cards on the foundations, favoring the left wing so long as cards there remain to be released.

**Wastepile**—Turn cards up from the hand one by one, placing unplayable cards face up on one wastepile. The top card of this pile, as well as the card in hand, is available for play on foundations.

# GAVOTTE

**(Odd and Even)**

Follow the rules for Royal Cotillion except: deal four rows of four cards each in both wings. Take your choice of which wing is to be totally available, and which is to have only bottom cards available. From the available cards choose your own foundations, two ranks in sequence. Each foundation is to be built up in skip-sequence until the pile contains thirteen cards.

# ROYAL RENDEZVOUS

All the kings and queens assemble in conclave if you win this pictorial solitaire.

**Layout**—Remove from the pack eight aces and four deuces, one of each suit. Place four aces of different suits in a row, and place remainder in a row below. Put two deuces on each side of the lower row. Then below the two rows deal two rows of eight cards each, forming the reserve. (See diagram.)

**Foundations**—The four upper aces are to be built up in suit and sequence to queens. The four lower aces are to be built up in suit and skip-sequence: A, 3, 5, 7, 9, J, K. The deuces are to be built up in suit and skip-sequence: 2, 4, 6, 8, 10, Q.

**Play**—Cards of the reserve are available for play on the foundations. Each space must be filled at once from the wastepile, if any, or from the hand.

Four kings are not built on foundations. These are to be put in a row above the aces, but no king may be so placed until another king of the same suit has been built on the lower row of aces.

**Wastepile**—Turn cards up from the hand one by one, placing unplayable cards in a single wastepile. The top card of this pile, as well as the card in hand, is available for play on foundations.

*Layout for Royal Rendezvous*

# SLY FOX

If there is any solitaire that can be licked by sheer skill against any luck of the cards, this is it. When you lose it, you can usually put your finger on an obvious mistake—if that's any comfort!

**Foundations**—Remove one ace and one king of each suit from the pack. Put them in two columns with space between for five more columns. (See diagram.) The aces are to be built up in suit to kings, and the kings down in suit to aces.

**Layout**—Deal twenty cards in four rows of five each, between the foundations. These cards start the wastepiles. Play up whatever you can on the foundations, filling each space at once from the hand.

**Play**—After play from the layout has come to a standstill, turn up cards from the hand, placing each either on a foundation or on any of the wastepiles. There is no restriction of choice on the wastepiles; you may place as many or as few additional cards as you wish upon any one pile. But having begun to deal, you must continue to do so until you have added twenty more cards to the wastepiles. Count the cards as they are turned, omitting the cards that are played upon foundations. Only after dealing the twenty additional cards, can plays again be made from wastepiles to foundations.

Continue adding twenty cards at a time to the wastepiles and pausing to play, until the pack is exhausted. (The last deal may be incomplete.) After the first layout has been replenished, do not fill any spaces except in the course of adding twenty more cards to the wastepiles.

*Layout for Sly Fox*

# MOUNT OLYMPUS

A pictorial solitaire, more interesting to play than many of this type. If won, Mount Olympus shows all the kings and queens dwelling on its slopes.

**Foundations**—Remove all the aces and deuces from the pack and arrange them in an arch or "mountain." (See diagram.) The suits and ranks may be alternated for pictorial effect. These foundations are to be built in suit, upward in skip-sequence, thus: A, 3, 5, 7, 9, J, K, and 2, 4, 6, 8, 10, Q.

**Tableau**—Deal nine cards in the form of a pyramid below the arch, forming the tableau. The top card of a tableau pile is always available for building on foundations or tableau. The tableau piles may be built in suit downward, in skip-sequence. A group of cards on top of a pile, in the same suit and correct sequence, may be moved in part or in whole.

Spaces in the tableau made by removal of an entire pile may be filled only from the hand. All spaces must be filled before the next deal.

**Hand**—Each time play comes to a standstill, with tableau spaces filled, deal nine more cards, one on each tableau pile.

**Helpful Hints**—Tableau piles must be examined frequently to keep track of reversed sequences (higher card dealt on a lower) and other sources of trouble. A more convenient layout for this purpose is to deal the tableau in one row, with the foundations in two rows above. Then the tableau can be spread in columns downward.

*Layout for Mount Olympus*

# FROG

Frog is one of the few solitaires that are almost entirely a matter of skill. As in Calculation and Sly Fox, you make your own destiny by shrewdness shown in placing cards.

**Layout**—Count thirteen cards face up into one pile. If any aces are turned up, place them to right of pile. Square up the pile of thirteen cards less aces, and place it at the left, forming the stock.

**Foundations**—If no ace was found in the stock, remove one ace from the pack. The eight aces are foundations, to be placed in a row beside the stock, as they become available, and to be built up to kings, regardless of suit. (See diagram.)

**Play**—Turn up cards one by one from the hand, placing unplayable cards on any of five wastepiles below the foundations. As many or as few cards may be put in one pile as desired. The only limitation is that no more than five piles may be made.

Available for play on foundations are the top card of the stock, the top card of each wastepile, and the card turned from the hand.

*Layout for Frog*

# FANNY

If Frog comes out too easily for your taste, try Fanny. This variant can pose you difficult problems—and sometimes there is no solution.

Follow all rules of Frog except: put twelve cards in the stock instead of thirteen. Do not throw aces out of the stock, nor remove an ace from the pack to commence the foundation row. All aces must be placed after becoming regularly available.

# COLORADO

The skill in most solitaire games—where there is opportunity for skill—lies in manipulating the tableau to make space. Colorado is unique in that a space is not an unmixed blessing, and skill consists in exercising restraint in making spaces.

**Layout**—Deal two rows of ten cards, forming the tableau.

**Foundations**—One ace and one king of each suit, as they become available, are to be placed in a row above the tableau. (See diagram.) The aces are to be built in suit up to kings, and the kings down in suit to aces.

**Play**—Top cards of tableau piles are available for play to foundations. A tableau card may not be moved for any other purpose. A space in the tableau must be filled at once by a card from the hand. Several cards may be played from the tableau, when each leaves a space, provided that all spaces are then duly filled. But no play from a pile of two or more cards is permitted while there is an open space anywhere.

Turn cards up from the hand one by one, placing each on a foundation, or on any one of the twenty tableau piles. These are in effect wastepiles. Once a card is turned from the hand, it must be placed before another play is made. The reason for this stringent rule is that the game is too easy if the player looks at the card from hand before deciding whether to make a space for it or lay it on a pile.

*Layout for Colorado*

# MATRIMONY

No doubt this solitaire was named from the way in which it is won, with the queens gaining ascendancy over the jacks.

**Foundations**—Remove one ♦Q and one ♦J from the pack and place them in column, jack above. All queens and jacks are foundations. The rest are to be put in position as they become available. Place the jacks in one row and the queens in a row below. (See diagram.) The jacks are to be built in suit down to queens; the queens in suit up to jacks.

**Layout**—Deal two rows of eight cards each, not overlapping. Play what you can on the foundations. In the diagram, move the ♣J and ♠Q into position, and build the ♦10 on the ♦J.

**Play**—Spaces in the tableau are not filled. Continue by dealing sixteen cards at a time on the sixteen piles or spaces, pausing after each deal to play up what you can.

After the entire pack is dealt and no further play can be made, pick up the last pile (at right end of lower row), and deal the cards singly on the tableau piles. Before dealing, turn this pile face down and place the first card in the space from which the pile was taken.

*Layout for Matrimony*

Then deal in order from the left end of the top row and play what you can.

Each time play comes to a standstill, deal out one tableau pile in the same way, taking the piles in order from last to first. If still blocked after each pile has been dealt once, game is lost.

# LA NIVERNAISE

**(Napoleon's Flank)**

One of the most popular of two-pack solitaires. The traditional rules give the player little control over his own destiny, and it is probable that they are liberalized by many players.

**Layout**—Deal two columns of four cards each, leaving space between for four additional columns. These eight cards form the flanks. If no ace or king is dealt, shuffle and deal again. The game is hopeless without an immediate space in the flanks.

Below the flanks, lay out a row of six piles of four cards each, forming the line. (See diagram, page 82.) Count off each group of four face down, square up the pile, and turn it face up, so that only the top card can be read.

**Foundations**—One ace and one king of each suit, as they become available, are to be moved into two rows between the flanks. The aces are to be built up in suit to kings, and the kings down in suit to aces.

**Play**—All cards in the flanks, and the top of every line pile, are available for play on foundations. Only as many cards in the line piles, from the top, may be examined as there are spaces in the flanks.

A space in the flanks may be filled by any available card from the line, but a space need not be filled until the player chooses. As a rule, at least one space should be kept open at all times, to be filled only when cards are released that will re-open the space.

A space in the line, by removal of an entire pile, must be filled at once by a group of four cards counted out face down from the hand and then turned face up.

**Hand**—When play comes to a standstill, add four more cards to each pile of the line from the hand. These cards must be counted off face down and turned up when squared, in deference to the rule as to examination of piles.

In the last round of dealing, however, when there may not be enough cards left to give each pile four cards, deal by rows so far as the cards will go, leaving them spread for examination.

*Layout for La Nivernaise*

**Reversal**—When the top cards of the two foundations of same suit are in sequence, one card may be transferred from one pile to the other.

**Redeal**—Two redeals are permitted. To redeal, pick up the line piles in reverse order, so that the pile at the right will be at the top of the new hand.

# TOURNAMENT

The rule of La Nivernaise as to examination of piles is difficult to follow without unintentional peeking. Furthermore, the rule leaves the player in the dark as to possible reversed sequences in the piles that will block the game, unless by chance he resolves them. Much more sensible—and still a good fight to win—is the variation, Tournament.

Follow rules of La Nivernaise except: deal the line by rows, overlapping the cards, so that all can be read. When two foundations of same suit are built to cards in sequence, any or all of one pile may be reversed upon the other, including the bottom cards.

# PARALLELS

If you find this too easy, check back and see whether you are following the rules of the deal. A little laxity is a wonderful help!

**Foundations**—Remove from the pack one ace and one king of each suit. The aces are to be built up in suit to kings, and the kings down in suit to aces.

**Layout**—Place the aces in a column at the left, the kings in a column at the right. Deal a row of ten cards between, starting the tableau. (See diagram.)

**Play**—The only building is upon the foundations, from tableau or hand. Play what you can from the first row of the tableau, filling each space at once from the hand. In the diagram, play the ♥Q on the ♥K and the ♦2 on the ♦A.

When there is no further play and the row is replenished, deal a second row of ten cards below the first, not overlapping. Both rows are now available. Build and fill spaces at once.

When play again comes to a standstill with both rows replenished, deal a third row of ten cards and continue in the same way to deal the pack by rows as far as it will go. But after the second deal observe these rules:

*Layout for Parallels*

All cards of the top and bottom rows are available, and play from these rows releases cards in the same columns of adjacent rows. The rule is simply that a card is available if it shows one free end. Spaces are filled from the hand, but remember that if any card is turned from the hand to fill a space, then all the spaces existing at that time must be filled. Furthermore, they must be filled in order from left to right, and by rows from top to bottom. The process may not be interrupted to make a play upon a foundation.

Suppose, with three rows dealt, a bottom card and the one above it are played off. When the space in the middle row is filled, the card may not be played off because the space below it must be filled also, and it becomes unavailable unless the lower card can be played first.

There is an option of playing as many cards as desired before filling spaces. They may be played one at a time from the outer rows, refilling at once. Thus, you see the next card from the hand before committing yourself as to the next play. Of course, you also keep the cards of the inner rows locked up, but there will be many times when you see that a released card would not be of immediate use anyhow.

When all rows are filled, the turn of the next card from the hand commits you to deal an additional row, and this row must be completed before another play is made.

**Reversal**—When the cards on top of the two foundation piles of same suit are in sequence, any or all cards from one pile may be reversed upon the other, except for the foundation ace or king.

# LABYRINTH

This game is not as intricate as it sounds. Nevertheless, there's a dragon lurking here that's not easy to slay.

**Foundations**—Remove one ace and one king of each suit from the pack and place them in a row. The aces are to be built up in suit to kings, and the kings down in suit to aces.

**Layout**—Deal a row of ten cards, commencing the tableau. Play what you can on the foundations, filling each space immediately from the hand. (See diagram.)

**Play**—When play comes to a standstill, deal a new row of ten cards on the tableau, below the row above. The bottom and top cards of every column are always available. Play from either end releases the next cards toward the middle. But spaces are filled only in the bottom row, which must be complete before another row is dealt.

*Layout for Labyrinth*

If two or more cards are played from the bottom of a column up, only the bottom card is replaced. Gaps opened in the middle of the tableau count for nothing. Only the ten cards at the bottom and top are available at all times.

After the pack is dealt, you may draw one card from anywhere in the tableau. This card is available, as well as the two cards on either side of the gap created by its removal. This is the only instance in which cards not at the top or bottom of a column become available.

# BABETTE

Babette is a deceptive jade. Just when you think you have her, she is apt to elude your grasp.

**Foundations**—One ace and one king of each suit are to be placed in a row above the tableau as they become available. The aces are to be built up in suit to kings, and the king foundations down in suit to aces. (See diagram, page 86.)

**Play**—Deal a row of eight cards. If any playable cards appear, put them in the foundation row. But do not fill spaces now, or at any other time. Continue dealing the pack in rows of eight, pausing after each deal to play what you can. Since spaces are not filled, gaps will presently appear in the columns. Keep track of where these gaps are.

Deal each new row so that it just overlaps the cards left in the previous row, but not any in a higher row.

Any card in the tableau is available if its lower end is not covered.

**Redeal**—Two redeals are permitted. To redeal, slide the columns of the tableau together and pick them up in reverse order to form a new hand.

***Layout for Babette***

# STAG PARTY

It is remarkable how the perplexities of this game are eased as the ladies are removed!

**Foundations**—All the 5's and all the 6's are foundations, to be put in place as they become available. Put the 5's in two columns at the left of the tableau, the 6's in two columns at the right. (See diagram.) The 5's are to be built in suit down to kings (following after aces); the 6's are to be built up in suit to jacks.

**Layout**—Deal a row of eight cards to start the tableau and play what you can. Continue by dealing out the whole pack in rows of eight, each overlapping slightly the row above, pausing after each deal to play what you can. Spaces made in the tableau are never filled.

**Play**—After each row is dealt, remove and discard any queens. Then play what you can on foundations. Since spaces are not filled, this process leaves gaps in the columns. The rows must be aligned with care so as to show just where these gaps are. The cards of a new row should be laid so as to overlap any cards left in the previous row, but not any cards of higher rows.

Any card in the tableau is available if its bottom end is not covered.

*Layout for Stag Party*

# FOUR INTRUDERS

If you don't win Stag Party often enough to suit you—or if you don't like to banish the ladies—try this one.

**Foundations**—Remove the eight aces from the pack and place them in a row, to be built up in suit to kings.

**Layout**—Deal four cards in a column at the left, forming the tableau. Then below the foundation row deal a row of eight cards, starting the reserve. (See diagram, page 88.)

The rest of the pack, except for the last four cards, is to be dealt to the reserve in rows of eight. Pause after each deal to play up what you can. Spaces are never filled. Any card in the reserve is available if its bottom edge is not covered.

**Play**—Tableau piles may be built down in suit as far as the ace. Available for building are tableau cards and free cards in the reserve. A whole tableau pile may be moved upon another, if the suit and sequence is correct. Spaces in the tableau are filled by any available cards from the reserve, and must be filled before the next deal to the reserve. Top tableau cards are available for building on foundations.

Place the last four cards of the pack in a column at the right. These cards are INTRUDERS. They are available for play on the foundations or tableau. The rule as to the reserve now changes so that reserve cards may still be played on the foundations, but not directly on the tableau. Spaces in the Intruder column are filled from the reserve, from which the cards may reach the tableau.

*Layout for Four Intruders*

# TRIUMPH

Don't be discouraged if you don't find much use for the tableau in the beginning—business picks up with the draws at the end.

**Foundations**—Remove the eight aces from the pack and place them in a row. These are foundations, to be built up in suit to kings.

**Layout**—Deal four cards in a column at the right, forming the tableau. Deal eight cards in a row below the foundations, starting the reserve. (See diagram.)

**Play**—Top cards of tablèau and reserve piles are always available for play on the foundations. Tableau cards may be built on each other in suit and down. A whole pile may be moved upon another, if the suit and sequence is correct. Spaces in the tableau are filled at once from the hand.

Reserve cards may be played only upon the foundations. Deal the hand in rows of eight upon the reserve piles, overlapping the cards in column. (The last row will usually be incomplete.) Pause after each deal to play up what you can. Spaces in the reserve must be filled from the hand, but may be filled one by one, with a pause to make any possible plays. The bottom card of each column is available. If all columns are filled, down to the last row dealt, the next

*Layout for Triumph*

card from the hand starts a new row, and the row must be completed before play is resumed.

After the pack has been dealt and play is at a standstill, draw any four cards from the reserve. A card drawn from any row above the bottom creates a gap, making card above the gap available. The four cards so drawn are also available. Any not placed on the foundations must eventually be distributed on the tableau piles, not more than one card to a pile. No further builds may be made on the tableau, other than with drawn cards.

Three such draws of four cards each are permitted. After each draw, play up available cards from the draw, the tableau, the bottom row of the reserve, and the gaps of the reserve. The game is lost if still blocked after the third draw.

# SENATE

### (Congress)

The temptation is strong in this game to shade the harsh rule on filling spaces—but come now, you wouldn't want to win every time, would you?

**Foundations**—Remove the eight aces from the pack and place them in a row, to be built up in suit to kings.

**Layout**—Below the foundations deal a row of eight cards, starting the reserve. At the right deal a column of four cards, starting the tableau. (Same as diagram for Triumph, page 89.)

**Play**—Tableau cards may be built on each other downward in suit. Available for building also are bottom cards of the reserve. A tableau pile may be moved as a whole for building on another. Spaces in the tableau are filled by available cards from the reserve. Top cards of the tableau are available for building on foundations.

**Reserve**—Deal the pack in rows of eight cards upon the reserve, each row overlapping the one above. Pause and play after each deal. Bottom cards of the columns are available for play upon foundations, tableau piles, or tableau spaces.

All spaces in the reserve must be filled from the hand before another complete row is dealt. The player has option of when to suspend play in order to fill spaces, but if any is filled all must be. Furthermore, spaces must be filled strictly in order: by rows from left to right, with rows taken in order from top to bottom.

After the hand is exhausted, no spaces in the reserve may be filled.

# BLOCKADE

The trick of this game is to keep one or two columns short and clear them away at the end. It is remarkable how far one space goes toward breaking up the blockade.

**Foundations**—Move the eight aces, as they become available, in a row above the tableau, to be built up in suit to kings.

**Play**—Deal a row of twelve cards, starting the tableau. Play up what you can. Tableau cards may be built down in suit. The top card of a tableau pile is always available for play on foundations or another pile. A group of cards on top of a pile, in correct sequence and suit, may be moved in whole or in part.

A space may be filled by any available card or group from the tableau, or by a card from the hand. At least one card must lie on each of the twelve spaces of the tableau before an additional row is dealt.

Whenever play comes to a standstill, deal a new row of twelve cards, one on each pile.

# MISS MILLIGAN

History does not record who Miss Milligan was, but if she invented this game, she earns praise for a pleasing blend of Klondike and Spider.

**Foundations**—The eight aces, as they become available, are to be placed in a row above the tableau and built up in suit to kings.

**Layout**—Deal a row of eight cards. If any aces and other playable cards appear, put them up. Do not fill spaces in this first row. Continue dealing eight cards at a time, overlapping the previous cards or filling in the spaces. Do not leave any gaps in the columns, and do not bother to align rows. (See diagram, page 92.) Just be sure to add one more card at the bottom of each column during the deal. Between deals, make what plays you can.

**Play**—The bottom cards of the columns are available for play on the foundations or on each other. They may be built downward in alternating colors. A group at the bottom of a column, in correct sequence, may be moved in whole or in part. In the diagram, the ♦7 may be moved on the ♠8, and then the two cards remaining in the seventh column may be moved on the ♦5.

A space left by removal of an entire column may be filled only

by an available king or an available build with a king at the bottom.
After the entire pack is dealt, one available card or group at a time may be lifted up and set aside. If these cards are eventually built correctly back on the tableau, or all played off on foundations, the privilege of "weaving" continues.

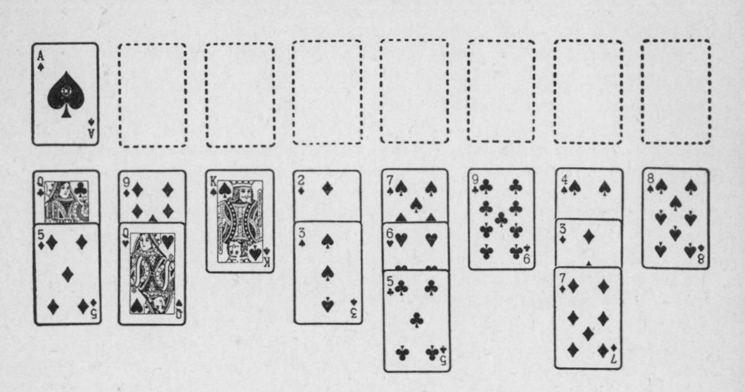

*Layout for Miss Milligan*

# SPIDER

The devotees of Spider, who are legion, claim it as the king of all solitaires. Certainly few others can give you quite the same combination of luck of the deal plus extraordinary opportunities to overcome bad luck by skillful manipulation.

**Layout**—Deal a row of ten cards face down. Add three more rows face down on the first. Deal four more cards face down, one on each of the first four piles. This makes in all forty-four cards face down. Now deal a row of ten face up on the piles. (Due to space limitations the diagram on the following page shows two rows of five cards instead of the normal layout of one row of ten cards.)

**Play**—All operations are carried out on the ten piles, which are at once tableau and foundations. The top card of each pile is available. Cards may be built on each other downward, regardless of suit. The sequence ends with the ace. The king may not be built on it.
A group on top of a pile, in correct sequence and also in suit, may

*Layout for Spider*

be moved in whole or in part. Hence there is a premium upon making the "natural" builds in suit, when possible.

On removing the last face-up card from a pile, turn up the top face-down card, which then becomes available.

A space made by removal of an entire pile may be filled by an available card or group. Kings may be moved only into spaces or into the discard.

The object of play is to assemble an entire suit of thirteen cards in ascending sequence from ace to king, from top card to bottom. Whenever a suit is so assembled and is available, it may be lifted off and discarded from the tableau. The game is won if all eight suits are so assembled and discarded.

An assembled suit need not be discarded until the player chooses. There may be advantage in breaking it up to help straighten other suits.

**Dealing**—After play on the original layout has come to a standstill, deal ten more cards, one on each pile. Continue in the same way, dealing a new row of ten cards and then pausing to play. Every space in the tableau must be filled before a new row is dealt.

# FORTY THIEVES

**(Napoleon at St. Helena, Big Forty, Roosevelt at San Juan)**

This game is probably the most widely known of two-pack solitaires. The original game is exasperatingly difficult to win. Many variations have been developed, designed to give the player a better chance.

**Layout**—Deal four rows of ten cards each, each row overlapping the one above. This is the tableau. (See diagram.)

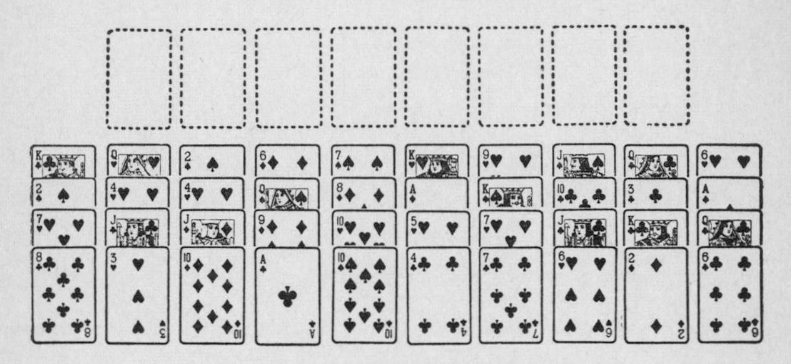

*Layout for Forty Thieves*

**Foundations**—The eight aces, as they become available, are to be moved to a row above the tableau and built up in suit to kings.

**Play**—The bottom card of each column of the tableau is available to be played on foundations or built on other piles. Only one card may be moved at a time. Tableau cards may be built down in suit. A space made by removal of an entire pile may be filled by any available card from tableau, wastepile, or hand.

**Wastepile**—Turn cards up from the hand one by one, placing unplayable cards face up on a single wastepile, which may be spread so that all cards can be read. The top card of the wastepile, as well as the card in hand, is available for play on foundations or tableau.

# LIMITED

Follow the rules of Forty Thieves except: deal the tableau in three rows of twelve cards each.

# LUCAS

Follow the rules of Forty Thieves except: put the eight aces in the foundation row first. Then deal the tableau in three rows of thirteen cards each.

# MARIA

Follow the rules of Forty Thieves except: deal the tableau in four rows of nine cards each. On the tableau piles, build down in alternate color.

# NUMBER TEN

Follow the rules of Forty Thieves, except: deal the first two rows of the tableau face down, the other two face up. On the tableau piles, build down in alternate color. A group on top of a pile, in correct sequence and alternation, may be moved in whole or in part.

# RANK AND FILE

**(Dress Parade)**

Follow the rules of Forty Thieves except: deal the first three rows of the tableau face down, the last face up. On the tableau, build down in alternating colors. A group on top of a pile, in correct sequence and alternation, may be moved in whole or in part.

# INDIAN

Follow the rules of Forty Thieves except: deal only three rows in the tableau, the first face down and the others face up. In building on the tableau, a card may be placed on the next highest card of any suit but its own.

# EMPEROR

Follow the rules of Forty Thieves except: deal the first three rows face down, the last face up. On the tableau piles, build down in alternate color. All face-up cards on a pile may be moved as a unit. Cards on foundation piles may be removed and built on the tableau.

# MIDSHIPMAN

Follow the rules of Emperor except: deal only thirty-six cards in four rows, the first two rows face down and the last two face up.

# OCTAVE

Follow the rules of Forty Thieves except: deal only twenty-four cards in three rows, the first two face down and the last face up. Below the tableau lay out a reserve of eight cards. On the tableau, build down in alternating colors. Reserve cards are available for tableau or foundation building, and spaces are filled from the hand. Cards may be turned from the hand so long as each can be built on foundations or tableau, or placed in a reserve space. The game is lost if non-usable card is turned.

# BUSY ACES

Many two-pack solitaires are elaborations of the classically simple Busy Aces.

**Layout**—Deal two rows of six cards each, forming the tableau. These cards may be built on each other downward in suit. Spaces may be filled from wastepile or hand. Top cards of tableau piles are available for play on foundations.

**Play**—The eight aces, as they become available, are to be placed in a row above the tableau and built up in suit to kings.

**Wastepile**—Turn up cards from the hand one by one, placing unplayable cards face up on a single wastepile. The top card of this pile, as well as the card in hand, is available for play upon foundations or tableau.

*Layout for Busy Aces*

# ROUGE ET NOIR

**(Red and Black)**

Like Busy Aces, Rouge et Noir is a basic type from which many other solitaires have been elaborated. The alternate color rule of building makes it much easier to win than Busy Aces.

**Foundations**—Remove the eight aces from the pack and place them in a row, to be built up in alternate colors to kings.

**Tableau**—Below the foundations deal a row of eight cards, forming the tableau. These cards may be built on each other downward in alternate color. Only one card at a time may be moved in building. The top card of a tableau pile is always available for play upon another pile or on foundations.

Spaces in the tableau may be filled only from the wastepile, if any, or hand.

**Wastepile**—Turn up cards from the hand one by one, placing unplayable cards face up in a single wastepile. The top card of this pile, as well as the card in hand, is available for play on foundations or tableau.

**Redeal**—One redeal is permitted. You may find that the redeal makes the game too easy for your taste. An alternative is to bar it, but allow tableau piles as a whole to be moved in building.

*Layout for Rouge et Noir*

# CONGRESS

**(President's Cabinet)**

Congress is one of the relatively few games in which foundation building is in suit, but tableau building disregards suit.

**Layout**—Deal two columns of four cards each, leaving room between the columns for two more columns. These eight cards start the tableau.

**Foundations**—The eight aces, as they become available, are to be moved into two columns in the center and built up in suit to kings.

**Play**—Cards in the tableau may be built downward, regardless of suit. The top card of a tableau pile is available for building on another pile or on foundations. Only one card at a time may be moved. Spaces in the tableau must be filled at once from the wastepile or hand.

**Wastepile**—Turn up cards from the hand one at a time, placing unplayable cards face up on a single wastepile. The top card of this pile, as well as the card in hand, is available for play on foundations or tableau.

*Layout for Congress*

# NAPOLEON'S SQUARE

There is plenty of scope here for clever manipulation to overcome the difficulties of a bad run of cards.

**Layout**—Deal twelve piles of four cards each around three sides of a square, leaving space in the center for eight cards. The piles may be dealt one card at a time in rotation, or four at a time. (See diagram.)

**Foundations**—The eight aces, as they become available, are to be moved to the center and built up in suit and sequence to kings.

**Play**—Tableau piles may be built downward in suit. The top card of a pile is always available for play on another pile, in a space, or on foundations. A group of cards on top of a pile, in correct suit and sequence, may be moved in whole or in part. A space in the tableau made by removal of an entire pile may be filled by any available card or group from the tableau, wastepile, or hand.

**Wastepile**—Turn cards from the hand one at a time, placing unplayable cards face up on a single wastepile. The top card of this

*Layout for Napoleon's Square*

pile, as well as the card in hand, is available for play on foundations, tableau piles, or tableau spaces.

Tableau piles may be spread for examination. A more convenient layout is to place aces in a row, the tableau piles in one or two rows below, with the cards spread downward in columns.

# BRITISH SQUARE

A difficult but interesting game, in which care must be exercised to avoid self-blocks by promiscuous building.

**Layout**—Deal four rows of four cards each, forming the tableau.

*Layout for British Square*

**Foundations**—One ace of each suit, as it becomes available, is to be moved into a row above the tableau. (See diagram.) Each ace is to be built in suit up to the king, then the second king is to be built on the first and in turn built down in suit to the ace.

**Play**—Tableau cards may be built on each other in suit, either up or down. But once a build is made, it fixes the direction of building for that pile; the direction may not be reversed on the same pile. But one pile may be reversed, card by card upon another of the same suit, if the foregoing rule is maintained.

Spaces in the tableau may be filled only from wastepile or hand. Top cards of tableau piles are available to be played on foundations.

**Wastepile**—Turn up cards from the hand one by one, placing unplayable cards face up on a single wastepile. The top card of the wastepile, as well as the card in hand, is available for play on foundations or tableau.

# FATHER TIME

**(Grandfather's Clock, Clock)**

A pictorial layout with a real purpose—it serves to show how far each foundation is to be built.

**Layout**—Remove from the pack the following twelve cards: ♣2, ♥3, ♠4, ♦5, ♣6, ♥7, ♠8, ♦9, ♣10, ♥J, ♠Q, ♦K. Arrange them in a circle to represent the hours of a clock, but place the ♣2 at "nine o'clock," and continue with the other cards in upward sequence. (See diagram.)

Around the rim of the clock deal twelve fans of three cards each, overlapping so that all cards can be read. These cards are the reserve.

**Foundations**—The twelve cards in the clock are foundations. Each is to be built up in suit until it reaches the number appropriate to its position. For example, the ♣2 is to be built up to 9, the ♥3 to 10, and so on. If the game is won, the piles in the positions of nine, ten, eleven (J), and twelve (Q) o'clock, will contain eight cards, the rest nine cards.

**Play**—Top cards of the reserve piles are available to be built on foundations and on each other. Building on the reserve is down in suit, the rank being circular. When a pile falls below three cards in size, it contains the corresponding number of spaces. The spaces must be filled from the hand (never from the wastepile). They need not be filled as they occur. The player has choice of when he shall suspend play to fill spaces. But if any space is filled, then all spaces existing at that time must be filled in proper sequence. Cards must be dealt to each short pile until it contains three cards, and the piles must be served clockwise beginning at "twelve o'clock."

**Wastepile**—Turn cards up from the hand one at a time, placing unplayable cards face up on a single wastepile. A card in hand is available to be played on foundations, built on a reserve pile, or filled in a reserve space. The top of the wastepile is available for building on foundations or reserve, but not for filling a space.

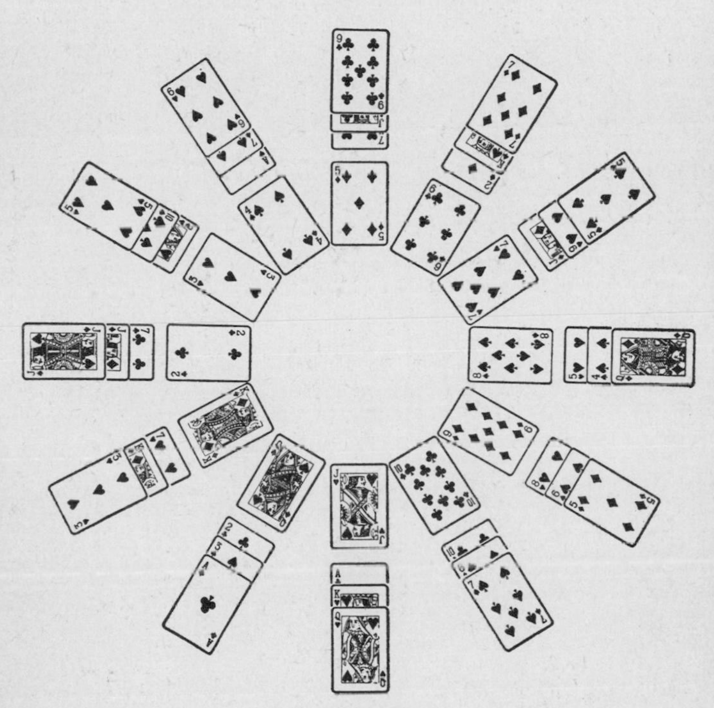

*Layout for Clock*

# HARP

Harp is Klondike played with two packs. It would be too easy if whole builds could be moved bodily, so the rule makes only the top card available.

**Layout**—Lay one card face up and beside it a row of eight cards face down. Deal the next card face up on the second pile, then deal seven more face down, one on each remaining pile. Continue in the same way so as to make nine piles, increasing in number from one to nine cards, with the top card of each pile face up and the rest face down. (See diagram.)

**Foundations**—The eight aces, as they become available, are to be placed in a row above the tableau and built up in suit to kings.

**Play**—Cards may be built on the tableau downward in alternating color. Only the top card of each tableau pile is available for building on the foundations or tableau. If the last face-up card is removed from a pile, turn up the top face-down card, which then becomes available.

A space in the tableau may be filled only by an available king, but for this purpose a group of cards on top of a pile, in proper sequence and alternation, with a king at the bottom, may be moved as a unit.

**Wastepile**—Turn up cards from the hand one by one, placing unplayable cards face up on one wastepile. The top card of the wastepile, as well as the card in hand, is available for play on foundations or tableau.

**Redeal**—There is no limit on redealing until the game is won or blocked.

*Layout for Harp*

# CONSTITUTION

The "track" principle of Parcheesi and Backgammon is applied in only a few solitaires, chief of which is Constitution. Under the rules stated below, you can be beaten only by an exceptionally bad layout, but you can beat yourself even with a good layout.

**Layout**—Remove from the pack all aces, kings, and queens. Place the aces in a row for foundations. Discard the kings and queens from the game. Below the aces deal four rows of eight cards each, forming the tableau. (See diagram.) Place the remainder of the pack face down to form the stock.

**Foundations**—The aces are to be built up in suit to jacks.

**Play**—Cards are playable to foundations only from the top row of the tableau. The cards in this row may be built on each other

*Layout for Constitution*

downward in alternating color. Available for building on the top row are also the cards of the second row. The top card of a build is available for play on a foundation, but never into a space.

A space in any row must be filled at once by moving up one card from the row below. The player has free choice of the card to move. The resultant space in the bottom row must be filled immediately by the top card of the stock. No builds may be made on the lower three rows of the tableau, and stock cards may not be played directly upon foundations. If no more spaces can be made to get additional stock cards into play, the game is lost.

# LIGHT AND SHADE

**(Red and Black, Alternates)**

In effect, Light and Shade is Constitution with the tableau cut in half both ways. The liberalization of foundation-building does not recompense for this drastic reduction in available cards, so that Light and Shade is much harder to win.

**Foundations**—Remove the eight aces from the pack and place them in a row, to be built up in alternate colors to kings.

**Tableau**—Below the foundations deal two rows of four cards each, forming the tableau.

*Layout for Light and Shade*

**Play**—Only the cards of the upper row are available for play upon the foundations and on each other. They may be built downward in alternate colors. The top card of a pile is always available, and one or all cards of the pile may be moved at once in building on the tableau.

Spaces in the upper row are filled only by cards moved up from the lower row. The player has free choice of the card to be moved. Spaces in the lower row must be filled at once from the wastepile, if any, or from the hand.

**Wastepile**—Turn cards from the hand one at a time, placing unplayable cards face up in a single wastepile. A card turned is available for play on foundations or tableau; once laid on the wastepile, a card is available only to fill a space in the lower row of the tableau.

# DEUCES

The traditional layout of Deuces is given here, but inveterate Patience players put foundations above, with the tableau in one or two rows below.

**Layout**—Remove the eight deuces from the pack and put them in two rows. These foundations are to be built up in suit to aces (coming after kings).

Deal ten cards around three sides of the foundations—a row of four above, and a column of three on each side. These ten cards are the tableau. (See diagram.)

*Layout for Deuces*

**Play**—Tableau piles may be built down in suit. The top card of a tableau pile is available for play on another, or on a foundation. Spaces in the tableau must be filled at once from the wastepile or hand, never from the tableau itself.

**Wastepile**—Turn up cards from the hand one at a time, placing unplayable cards face up in one wastepile. The top card of this pile, together with the card in hand, is available for play on foundations or tableau.

**Redeal**—One redeal is permitted.

# SQUARE

Follow all the rules for Deuces except: (a) do not remove the deuces from the pack at the beginning. Move them into position as they become available. (b) Increase the number of tableau piles to twelve.

# HERRINGBONE

This game is one of the many pictorial solitaires that were popular years ago. The trend now is to concentrate on the battle and skip the scenery.

**Foundations**—All eight jacks, as they become available, are to be placed in a column and built in suit down to aces.

**Tableau**—Deal six cards in any convenient formation. These tableau cards may be built on each other upward in suit. Fill spaces in the tableau from the wastepile, never from the tableau itself. The top tableau cards are available to be played on foundations.

**Play**—Turn up cards from the hand one by one, placing unplayable cards face up on a single wastepile. The top card of this pile, as well as the card in hand, is available for play on foundations or tableau.

Kings and queens are discarded from play when available. Each is to be placed beside a jack of its suit, kings on the left, and queens on the right. The discard may not be made until a jack is in place for the king or queen to match. The kings and queens are turned at an angle to make the herringbone pattern. (See diagram, page 109.)

**Redeal**—One redeal is permitted.

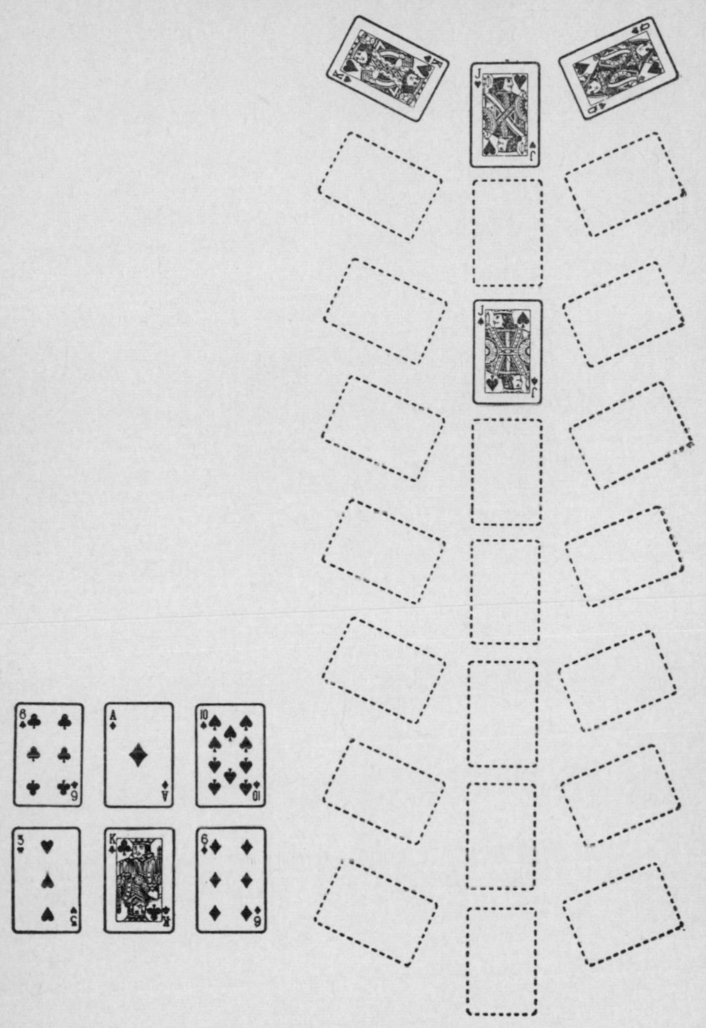

*Layout for Herringbone*

# GRAND DUCHESS

The right to scavenge the reserve, plus four deals, may seem to be an unduly generous concession to your will to win. But there is more in this game than meets the eye.

**Foundations**—One ace and one king of each suit, as they become available, are to be placed in two rows above the tableau. The aces are to be built up in suit to kings, and the king foundations are to be built down in suit to aces.

**Play**—Deal a row of four cards face up to start the tableau, and then deal two in a pile face down to start the reserve. (See diagram.) Play what you can from tableau to foundations and continue dealing in the same way—four cards to the tableau, one on each pile, then two face down to the reserve.

Top cards of the tableau are available for play on the foundations. Spaces in the tableau may never be filled, except in the course of the next deal.

After the hand is exhausted, turn over the reserve, spread it, and pick all the cards that can be played up on the foundations.

*Layout for Grand Duchess*

Continue play from the tableau as well, if the reserve cards make new plays possible.

**Redeals**—Three redeals are permitted. To redeal, pick up the tableau piles in reverse order, with the last pile at the top of the new hand, and put the remainder of the reserve at the bottom. In the last redeal, do not place any cards on the reserve pile; deal all four at a time, on the tableau.

# PARISIENNE

Parisienne is Grand Duchess except that the eight foundations are taken from the pack and placed before the first deal.

# DIPLOMAT

**(Rows of Four)**

This one is an easy puzzle of the Streets and Alleys type. You should solve it three times out of four.

*Layout for Diplomat*

**Layout**—Deal a column of four cards at the extreme left to start the left wing of the tableau. Then deal a column of four a little to right of the center, starting the right wing. Continue dealing four cards at a time alternately to the two wings, overlapping each column upon the one previously dealt. Deal four columns, totaling sixteen cards, to each wing. (See diagram.)

**Foundations**—The eight aces, as they become available, are to be placed in two columns between the wings, and are to be built up in suit to kings.

**Play**—Tableau cards may be built downward, regardless of suit. Spaces in the tableau may be filled by any available cards, which are the top cards of tableau piles (right end of each row), top card of the wastepile, and cards turned from the hand. All are available to be played on foundations, built on the tableau, or put in spaces.

**Wastepile**—Turn up cards from the hand one by one, placing unplayable cards face up on the wastepile. The top card of the wastepile, as well as the card in hand, is available for play on foundations or tableau.

**Redeal**—One redeal is permitted.

# QUEEN OF ITALY

**(Terrace)**

Little-exploited among solitaires is the allowing of choice of foundation. Here it is built up into a neat opportunity for skill.

**Layout**—Deal a row of eleven overlapping cards, forming the reserve. Deal three cards and choose one of them for a foundation, after examining the reserve to guide your choice. Place the foundation at the left to start another row under the reserve. Place the remaining two cards to start a third row under the foundation. Complete the bottom row by dealing seven more cards, making nine in all. These cards, which start the tableau, should not be overlapped. (See diagram.)

**Tableau**—Top cards of tableau piles are available for play on foundations and upon each other. Tableau cards may be built down in alternate colors, but only one card at a time may be moved from a tableau pile. Spaces in the tableau must be filled at once from the wastepile or hand, never from the tableau.

**Play**—All other cards of same rank as the selected foundation card are to be moved into the foundation row as they become available.

*Layout for Queen of Italy*

The foundations are to be built up in alternate colors, until each comprises thirteen cards. Ace and king are in sequence. Thus, if a 3 is selected, each foundation must be built from 3 to king, then ace and deuce.

**Reserve**—The reserve cards may be played only on foundations. They are available one at a time, from right to left.

# BLONDES AND BRUNETTES

**(Brunette and Blonde)**

This solitaire is Queen of Italy with the choice left out. Follow all the rules of that game except: deal only ten cards in the reserve. After laying out the reserve and the tableau of nine cards, deal the next card for the first foundation. There is no redeal.

# PLOT

The stock in this game is concealed underground and hard to penetrate. The rule of the first foundation compels the conspirators to plan their work well.

*Layout for Plot*

**Layout**—Count off thirteen cards face down, square them up, and place them face up to form the stock. Deal the next card far to the left for the first foundation. Below the stock, deal three rows of four cards each, forming the tableau. (See diagram.)

**Foundations**—The other seven cards of same rank as the first foundation are foundations also, to be placed in two columns of four on either side of the tableau.

**Play**—Each foundation is to be built up, regardless of suit, to thirteen cards. Sequence of rank is circular. In the diagram, the ♥10 is the first foundation. The sequence on each foundation will be 10, J, Q, K, A, 2, and so on, to 9.

No other foundation may be moved into the columns until the first foundation has been built up to thirteen cards. As soon as it is complete, however, all remaining foundations may be moved into place from the tableau, stock, wastepile, and hand.

The top card of the stock is available to be played only on a foundation.

**Tableau**—The top card of each tableau pile is available to be played only on a foundation. Cards from wastepile and hand may be built on tableau piles downward, regardless of suit. But a foundation card breaks the sequence; it can not be built on a higher card, and a lower card may not be built upon it.

Until the first foundation is complete, a space in the tableau may be filled only by a foundation card from wastepile or hand. After the first foundation is complete, a space may be filled by any card from wastepile or hand, but never by a card already in the tableau.

**Wastepile**—Turn up cards from the hand one by one, placing unplayable cards face up on a single wastepile. The top card of the wastepile, as well as the card in hand, is available for play on foundations or tableau, and in tableau spaces subject to the foregoing restrictions.

# CORNERSTONES

### (Four Corners)

Watch your building, or you kill your own chances in this game.

**Layout**—Deal two columns of six cards each, leaving space between for two columns of foundations. Turn the top and bottom cards of the columns lengthwise. These are cornerstones. Continue dealing the whole pack in the same order upon the twelve cards laid out, pausing to play when possible. These piles are the tableau. (See diagram, page 116.)

**Foundations**—One ace and one king of each suit must be placed as soon as turned up from the hand. The ace and king of the same suit must be placed side by side in the central area, aligned with one row of the tableau other than the cornerstones. Strictly, the first foundation must be placed in the top row, the next of a different suit in the second row, and so on. But you may give yourself the slight advantage of a choice in placing the first three suits.

The aces are to be built up in suit to kings, the kings in suit down to aces.

**Play**—In dealing the tableau, inspect cards from the hand as they turn up and place suitable ones on foundations. Do not skip any tableau piles in dealing, because of such play: deal one card to each pile in turn until the pack is exhausted. But there is a restriction on the play during the deal.

Cards that would fall upon cornerstones may be played anywhere in the center, but a card that would fall on any other pile may be played only on the row of that pile. For example, in the diagram the ♥Q may not be moved upon the ♥K because it was dealt in the club row.

After the pack is exhausted, the rules change. Top cards of all tableau piles are available for play anywhere. Available cards may also be built on each other, in suit, either up or down, and the sequence in the suit is circular for this purpose.

When the top cards of two foundations of the same suit are in sequence, any or all cards of one pile may be reversed upon the other, except that the bottom card of a pile may not be moved.

**Redeal**—Two redeals are permitted. To redeal, pick up the tableau piles in reverse of the order in which they were dealt, making a new hand. (The lower right corner stone should thus be at the top of the new hand.) Deal the tableau again, following rules of the original deal.

*Layout for Cornerstones*

# ST. HELENA

**(Napoleon's Favorite, Washington's Favorite, Privileged Four)**

This is supposed to have been the solitaire with which Napoleon beguiled the days of his last exile. Too bad he didn't leave us some pointers for Patience players comparable to his maxims on military strategy.

**Foundations**—Remove one ace and one king of each suit from the pack and arrange them in two rows. The ace foundations are to be built up in suit to kings, and the king foundations are to be built down in suit to aces.

**Layout**—Deal the rest of the pack into twelve piles, arranged in a rectangle around the foundations. Place the first pile above the left card in the column of foundations, then go clockwise. There should be four piles in the top line of the tableau, four in the bottom line, and two in column at each side. (See diagram.)

**Play**—Only the top cards of the tableau piles are available. They may be built upon each other, moving one at a time, either up or down, and regardless of suit, but the sequence is not circular. Only a queen may be built on a king, and only a deuce on an ace.

*Layout for St. Helena*

In this first deal, there is a restriction on the play to foundations. The top four piles of the tableau may be played upon king foundations only, while the bottom line may feed only the aces. From the side piles, cards may be moved anywhere.

**Redeal**—Two redeals are permitted. To redeal, pick up the piles counterclockwise, beginning with the last (upper pile of the left side), making a new hand. Deal again into twelve piles as far as the cards will go.

In the redeals there is no longer any restriction on the play to the foundations. The top card of any tableau pile may be moved to any other one, or to any foundation.

# BOX KITE

It cannot be denied that redealing a double pack of cards is laborious. Here is a variant of St. Helena that skips the redeals by liberalizing the rules of play.

**Layout**—Place eight foundations and deal out the pack as in St. Helena.

**Play**—Top cards of all tableau piles are available for play upon any other pile or on any foundation. Build up or down, regardless of suit, on tableau piles. Here the sequence is circular (ace and king consecutive). A space in the tableau may not be filled.

**Reversal**—When the top cards on the two foundations of same suit are in sequence, any or all cards of one pile may be reversed upon the other, except for the ace or king at the bottom.

# LOUIS

**(St. Louis, Newport)**

On the other hand, perhaps you like to labor hard for your wins. Louis is St. Helena made tougher. Follow all the rules of St. Helena with the following exceptions:

After laying down the first twelve cards of the tableau, play what you can on the foundations, filling spaces from hand. Then deal the rest of the pack without playing, until the deal is complete.

All top tableau cards are available for play anywhere.
Building on the tableau piles may be up or down, but must be in suit.

# CAPRICIEUSE

The name, no doubt, is an allusion to the patron saint of Patience, Lady Luck. Here she is likely to be kinder than in Louis, which is in effect the same game with less play during the deal.

**Foundations**—Remove one ace and one king of each suit from the pack, and place these foundations in a row. The aces are to be built up in suit to kings, and the kings down in suit to aces.

**Layout**—Deal the rest of the pack into twelve piles in two rows of six. (See diagram.)

**Play**—During the deal, place on a foundation any suitable card turned up from the hand. Do not skip piles in dealing because of such play: give one card to each pile in turn. Only the card in hand may be played up. Once placed on a tableau pile, a card is not available until the deal is finished.

After the deal, top cards of tableau piles are available for play on foundations or on each other. Building on the tableau is in suit,

*Layout for Capricieuse*

but may go up or down. The sequence is not circular; only a deuce may be placed on an ace, only a queen on a king.

**Redeal**—Two redeals are permitted. To redeal, pick up the piles in reverse of the order in which they were dealt to form a new hand.

# LEONI'S OWN

A game of fascinating variety. The method of counting out the Exiles is used in itself without trimmings to make several solitaires and gambling games.

**Foundations**—Remove one ace and one king of each suit from the pack, and place these foundations in two rows. The aces are to be built up in suit to kings, and the kings down in suit to aces.

**Layout**—Deal the rest of the pack into thirteen piles as far as it goes, forming the tableau. Consider the piles to be numbered from one to thirteen, or Ace to King. (See diagram.) When any card turned from the hand is of same rank as the pile to which it would be dealt, set it aside instead, face down in a special pile at the left. The cards placed are Exiles. Do not skip any tableau piles in dealing because of an exile; the next card of the pack takes the place of an exile, and each pile receives a card in turn.

*Layout for Leoni's Own*

**Play**—Spread the cards of the thirteen or King pile. All these cards are available for play on the foundations, together with the top cards of the other twelve piles. Play up what you can, and whenever play comes to a standstill, turn up the top card of the exiles. If this card is playable on a foundation, it must be so played, and the next exile card turned. If it cannot be played, put it under the tableau pile of its own rank, remove the top card of that pile, and put it under the pile of its rank, and so on. Continue shifting cards in this manner until a playable card is uncovered at the top of a tableau pile. After putting the card just removed under the proper pile, play up the disclosed card together with any others now suitable.

When the exile card, or any other reached in shifting, is a king, it stops the play. The king must be placed under the King pile and a new exile card turned.

**Reversal**—When the top cards of the two foundations of same suit are in sequence, any or all cards of one pile may be reversed upon the other, except for the ace or king at the bottom of the pile.

**Redeal**—Two redeals are permitted after the exiles are used up and play comes to a standstill. Pick up the tableau piles in reverse order, so that the King pile will be at the top of the new hand. Deal exactly as at first, exiling cards that would fall on the pile of their own rank.

The rule that an exile or a card disclosed by a shift must be played if possible does not apply to two foundations at the reversible stage. The player can circumvent the rule anyhow by reversing enough cards to preclude the play. The cards can later be reversed back if desired.

# CRESCENT

A game of reverses—but don't blame bad luck if you find yourself blocked by a reverse sequence of your own making.

**Foundations**—Remove one ace and king of each suit from the pack and arrange these foundations in two rows. The aces are to be built up in suit to kings, and the king foundations are to be built down in suit to aces.

**Layout**—Deal the rest of the pack into sixteen piles of six cards each, arranged in a semicircle around the foundations, forming the tableau. Deal the first five cards of each pile face down, the last face up. (See diagram, page 122.)

**Play**—Top cards of tableau piles are available for play on foundations or on each other. Tableau building is in suit, but may go up

*Layout for Crescent*

or down, and the sequence is circular (ace and king consecutive). If all the face-up cards are removed from a pile, turn the next card face up. Spaces in the tableau may not be filled.

**Reversal**—When the top cards of two foundations of the same suit are in sequence, any or all cards of one pile may be reversed upon the other.

**Shifts**—When play upon the original layout is blocked, take the bottom card of each pile and place it face up on top. Then continue play. Three such shifts are permitted. Note that every bottom card must be moved to the top during the shift, even where all cards of a pile are face up.

# HOUSE IN THE WOOD

This is La Belle Lucie with two packs, but what a difference! The one-pack game is blocked nine times out of ten by an unlucky third deal. Though restricted to one deal, this game can be won nine times out of ten, assuming you don't destroy it with your own hand.

**Layout**—Distribute the cards face up in thirty-four fans of three cards each and one fan of two. (See La Belle Lucie, page 42, for diagram.)

**Foundations**—All aces are foundations to be put in a row as they become available, and to be built up in suit to kings.

**Play**—Only the top card of each fan is available. Available cards may be built on foundations, or upon each other in suit, up or down. Only a queen may go on a king and only a deuce on an ace. If all cards of a fan are removed, it is not replaced. There is no redeal and no reversal on foundation piles.

# HOUSE ON THE HILL

Follow the rules for House in the Wood except regarding foundations. Here the foundations are one ace and one king of each suit, placed as they become available. Aces are to be built up in suit to kings, and king foundations down in suit to aces.

# INTELLIGENCE

A European variation of La Belle Lucie, generally called Patience Intelligent, in tribute to its opportunity for skill.

**Layout**—Deal eighteen fans of three cards each. (See La Belle Lucie, page 42, for diagram.) If any aces are turned up in dealing, place them at once in the foundation row and replace them with the next cards.

**Foundations**—All eight aces, as they become available, are to be moved into a row and built in suit up to kings.

**Play**—Only the top card of each fan is available. Available cards may be built on foundations, or on each other in suit, either up or down. If all cards of a fan are removed, fill the spaces by a new fan of three cards from the hand. This is the only way the cards from the hand may be brought into play.

**Redeal**—Two redeals are permitted. When play comes to a standstill, gather all cards exclusive of foundation piles, shuffle them thoroughly, and deal a new layout. During redeals, aces may be put in the foundation row, but no other builds may be made until the deal is complete.

*Layout for Olga*

# FOUR-PACK SOLITAIRES

## OLGA

A game strictly for players who are not staggered by a huge layout and a wealth of building possibilities.

**Pack**—From each of four packs discard the deuces, 3's, 4's, 5's, and 6's. The remaining cards rank normally from king high down to 7, with aces below 7's.

**Layout**—Deal seven rows of seven cards each, all cards separate. The second, fourth, and sixth rows should be face down, all others face up. These forty-nine cards are the tableau.

**Foundations**—The sixteen aces, as they become available, are to be placed in two columns on either side of the tableau and built in suit up to kings. (See diagram.) Any aces turned up in dealing the tableau may be moved at once to the foundation columns, and any suitable card turned in dealing may be built on an established foundation. But a card once laid down in the tableau may not be moved until the tableau is complete.

**Play**—Face up cards in the tableau may be built on each other downward in alternate colors. All cards of a tableau pile may be moved as a unit upon another pile. Spaces may be filled by any available top card from wastepile, hand, or another tableau pile. All tableau cards are available for tableau building, but only the bottom cards of the columns are available for building on foundations. When a face-down card becomes exposed at the bottom of a column, it is turned face up and becomes available.

**Wastepile**—Turn cards up from the hand one by one, placing unplayable cards face up on a single wastepile. The top card of this pile, as well as the card in hand, is available for building on tableau or foundations.

## EMPRESS OF INDIA

This game is complex as to both the layout and the rules, but with scope for plenty of maneuver in timing the use of spaces.

**Pack**—Shuffle together four complete packs, making 208 cards in all.

*Layout for Empress of India*

**Layout**—Remove the eight black queens, the eight red jacks, the eight red kings, and the eight black aces. Place the queens in a single pile in the center, with a ♣Q on top, and place the red jacks in a circle around the pile. These sixteen cards are purely ornamental, the ♣Q representing the Empress of India and the red jack her guards. Put the black aces and red kings in two concentric circles around the Empress and guards. (See diagram.)

Deal four rows of twelve cards each. The upper two rows, representing the Army, must be all red, and the lower two, the Navy, all black. In dealing the rows, place each card turned up in the section of its proper color, and if any excess of one color is turned up, place these cards face up in a wastepile.

**Foundations**—The black aces are to be built up in suit to kings, and the red kings are to be built down in suit to aces. Owing to the absence of the ornamental cards, the sequences will be:

| *Black* | *Red* |
|---|---|
| A | K |
| 2 | Q |
| 3 | 10 |
| 4 | 9 |
| 5 | 8 |
| 6 | 7 |
| 7 | 6 |
| 8 | 5 |
| 9 | 4 |
| 10 | 3 |
| J | 2 |
| K | A |

The rows of this tabulation give corresponding cards (see below).

**Foundation Building**—Cards may be played upon the foundations only in pairs of corresponding cards (see table), one red and one black. Only the cards in the Army and Navy are available for transfer to foundations. Spaces in the tableau are filled from the wastepiles or hand, and cards from these sources can reach the foundations only by way of the Army and Navy.

**Tableau Building**—To make a space in the tableau, an Army card may be built upon the corresponding Navy card, or vice versa. Such paired cards may be subsequently moved only to be built simultaneously on foundations.

**Wastepiles**—Turn up cards from the hand one by one, placing them face up in two wastepiles, one of red cards and the other of black. Since these cards can be brought into play only to fill spaces in the Army and Navy, spaces should not be made by building until it is seen that the available wastepile cards will be useful.

# MULTIPLE SOLITAIRE

Any solitaire may be played as a competitive game among two or more persons. Following are the three chief methods.

**Comparative Scoring**—Each player has his own pack or packs, and plays his own game. After each player has finished, by winning his game or coming to a standstill, the scores are compared. The score is usually the number of cards built on foundations, but it may be some other quantity if the game is not one of foundation-building. It may be agreed that a competition will comprise a prefixed number of games. Special systems of this kind are described in connection with Golf and Pyramid.

**Common Foundations**—The comparative scoring method may be combined with the idea of playing on common foundations. Each player has his pack or packs, and his own layout, but the foundations are common to all and are built on by all the players. After the game comes to a standstill, the foundation piles are sorted out and the number of cards belonging to each player is counted. Widely popular is multiple Klondike using this system.

**Identical Cards**—Cribbage Squares, Poker Squares, and like games lend themselves to a very effective test of skill among a number of players. Each has his own pack. One player appointed as "caller" shuffles his pack and then turns cards up one by one, announcing the suit and rank of each. Each other player, having sorted his pack into suits for convenience, picks out the called card and puts it into position as he pleases in his own tableau. Thus, all the tableaux comprise the same sixteen or twenty-five cards, and the player with the highest count wins.